AF568089

GURU DUTT
THROUGH LIGHT AND SHADE

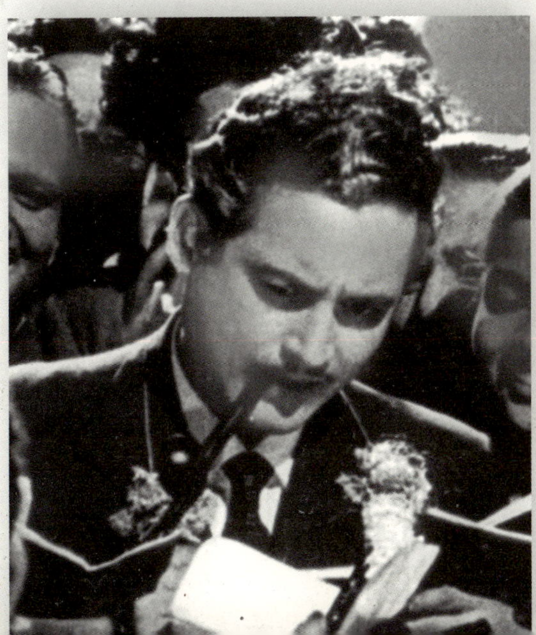

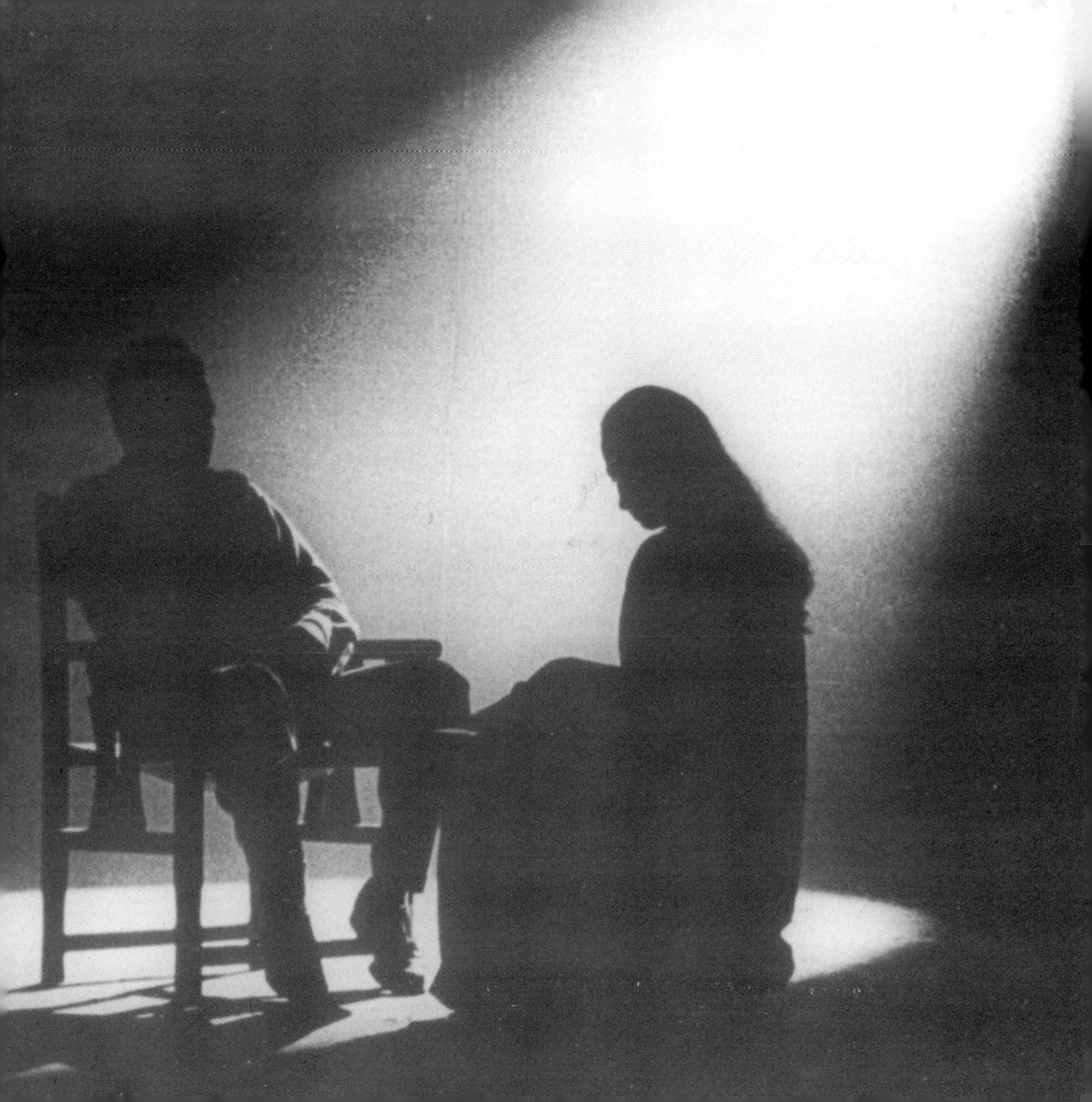

GURU DUTT
THROUGH LIGHT AND SHADE

RASHMI DORAISWAMY

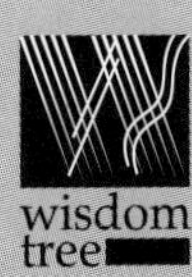

Photographs courtesy: Osian's Connoisseurs of Art and National Film Archives of India

ISBN 978-81-8328-107-2

Published by
Wisdom Tree
4779/23 Ansari Road
Darya Ganj
New Delhi – 110002
Ph: 23247966/67/68

Published by Shobit Arya for Wisdom Tree; *edited by* Manju Gupta; *designed by* Kamal P. Jammual; *typeset at* Marks and Strokes, New Delhi-110002 and *printed at* Print Perfect, New Delhi-110064

CONTENTS

	Editor's Note	*vii*
	Acknowledgements	*xi*
1.	Introduction	1
2.	The Golden Fifties	7
3.	Issues of Authorship	29
4.	Narratives of Homelessness	57
5.	Passing through Light, Passing through Shadows	91
	Songs	105
	Filmography	109

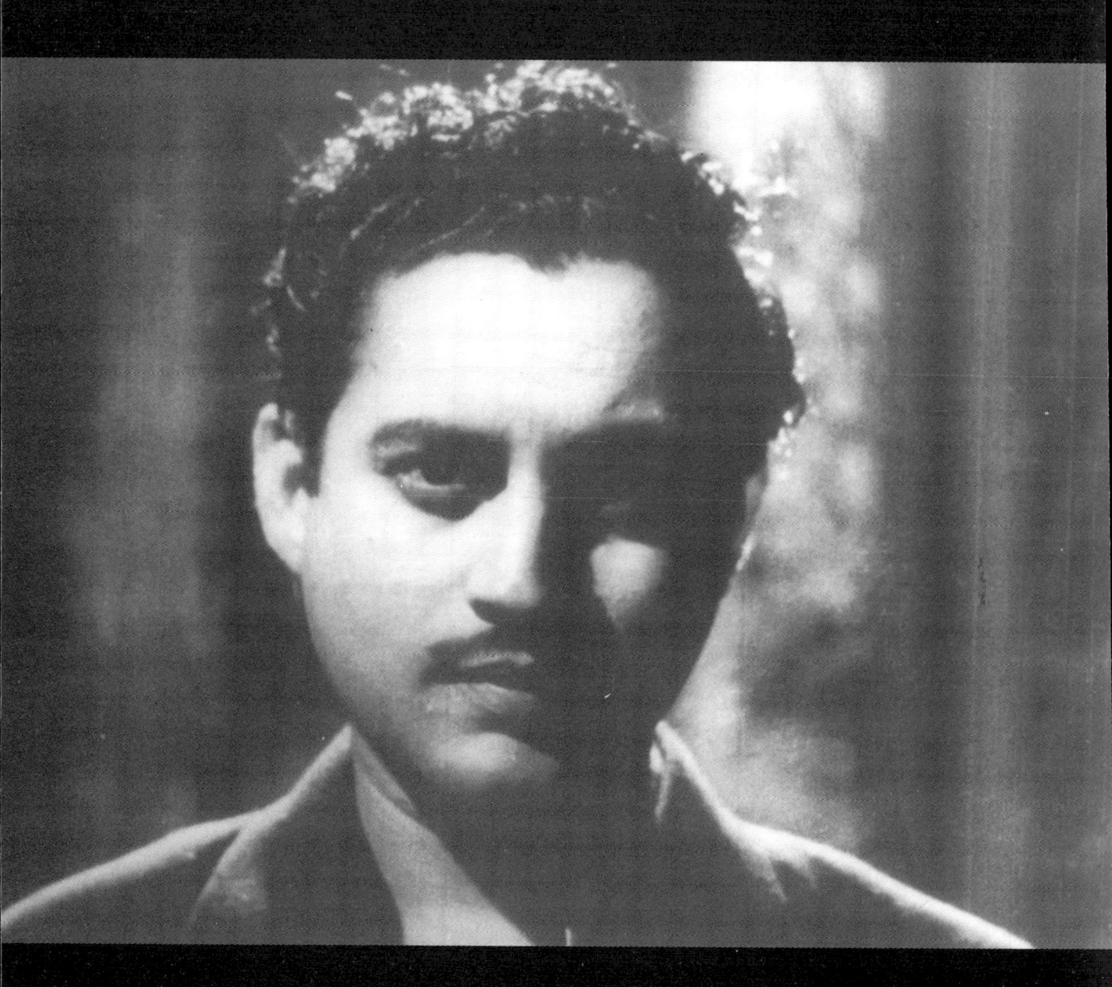

Guru Dutt in *Mr & Mrs 55*

EDITOR'S NOTE

Much has been written about Guru Dutt, the 'melancholy poet of Indian cinema', 'the solitary existentialist', the romantic hero consumed by the pain of living. In *Pyaasa*, the most consummate of the films he made and acted in, he achieved a tragic stature.

His life as much as his oeuvre is the stuff that legends are made of. But Guru Dutt was much greater than the myths that have grown up around him. He directed and/or acted in only a few films – two of the biggest successes he produced – *Chaudvin ka Chand* and *Sahib, Bibi aur Ghulam* which were 'directed' by his friends M. Sadiq and Abrar Alvi respectively, but bear the unmistakeable stamp of his hand and are generally considered a part of the too-small body of his work.

Like many great artistes (Ritwik Ghatak among them), he remained unsung in his lifetime. The last film he lent his name to as director, *Kaagaz ke Phool*, was a box- office disaster and he vowed never to put his name as director to another. Ironically, it was *Chaudhvin ka Chand* and *Sahib, Bibi aur Ghulam* which followed, achieving the resounding success that eluded the films he had directed earlier. His premature death, before he was 40, was widely regarded as suicide. Success came later—huge success, national and international. In the Hindi cinema in Bombay, the Golden Period is acknowledged as the fifties, and it belongs indisputably to Raj Kapoor, Bimal Roy, Mehboob Khan and Guru Dutt. Very different, one from the other, they shared a worldview informed by a rage against a system that separated the rich from the poor, a deep commitment to human values and enormous talent as filmmakers, whether as directors or actors (or both), and sometimes even as producers.

Today Guru Dutt is revered and recognised as a 'master'

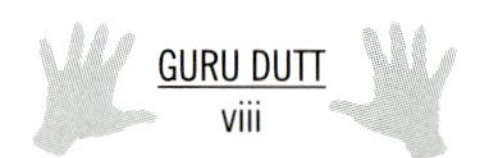

not only in India, but everywhere in the world where cinema is recognised as an art. Retrospectives of his works are shown in film festivals all over the world; scores of articles, books and monographs about him, abound. A film has been made about him as well.

So why did we need yet another book on Guru Dutt? Because **Rashmi Doraiswamy**, who is a scholar and an author, looks not only at his life and his career — both of which have been widely written about, she analyses his films from a different perspective, making few concessions to popular myths or tastes, choosing to look at the distinguishing marks of his authorship — the recurring motifs in his films which he directed or produced, his use of space, his song picturisations, the manner in which his films are structured, and more. In writing about Guru Dutt's films, it reveals the art of cinema itself.

Aruna Vasudev
Series Editor

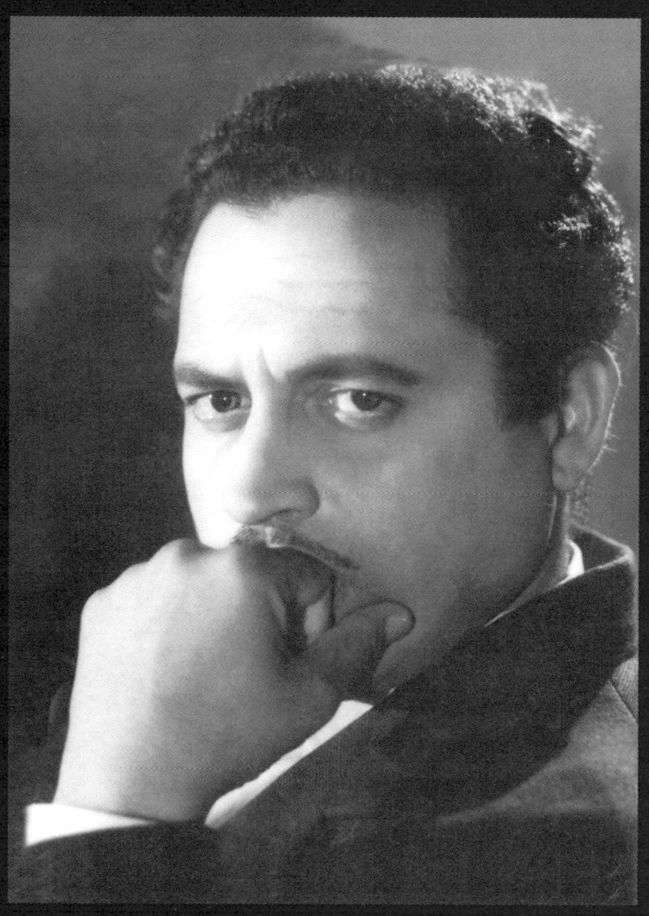

Guru Dutt in *Kaagaz ke Phool*

ACKNOWLEDGEMENTS

I am grateful to Aruna Vasudev for having encouraged me to apply for the MAJLIS Research Fellowship in 1999. I received the fellowship from January to December 1999 to work on a project entitled 'The Changing Narrative Strategies of Hindi Cinema'. This volume consists of excerpts from the unpublished manuscript of the project.

Without the constant support that my parents, brother, husband and children provided, this book would not have been possible.

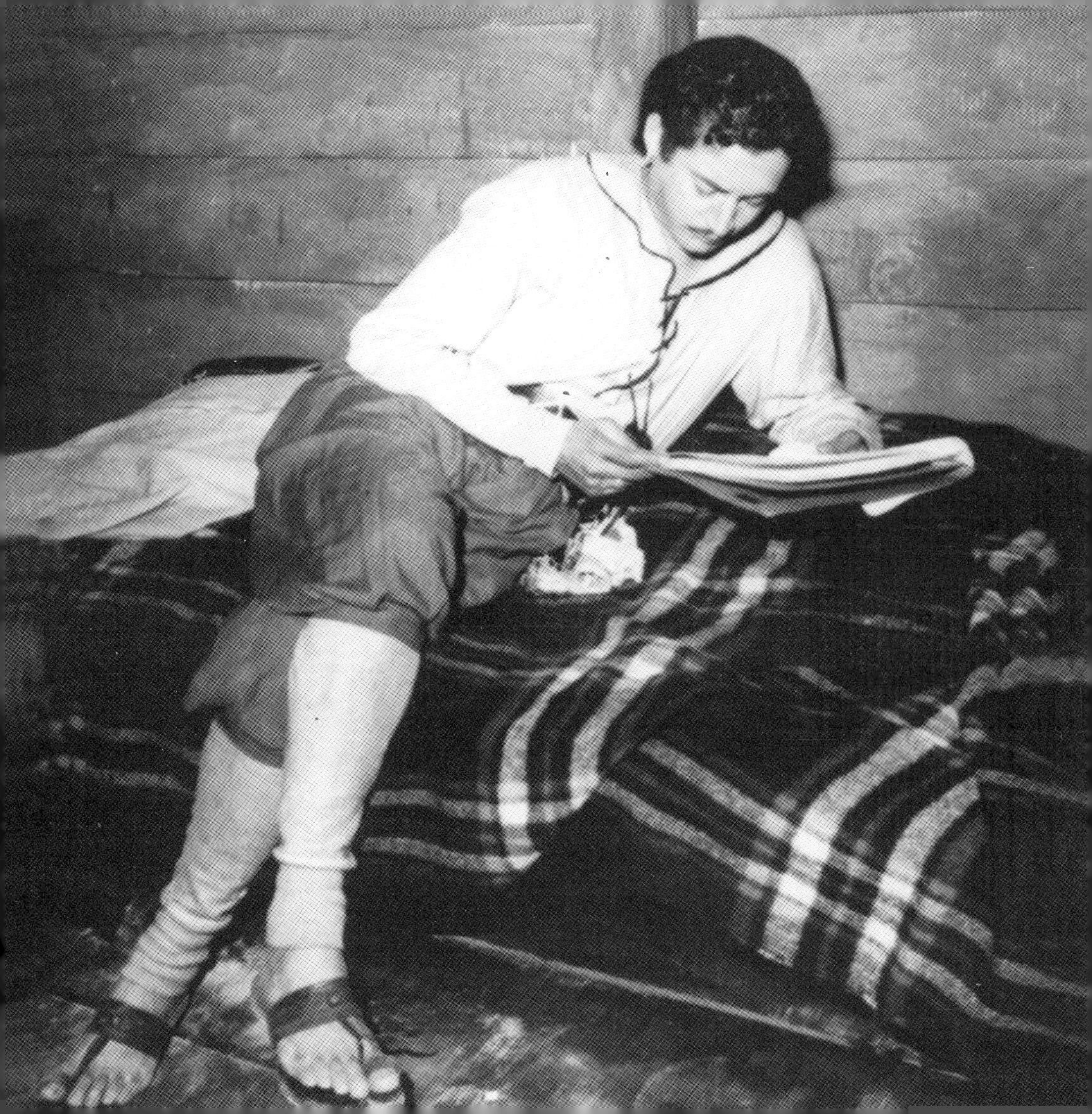

1

INTRODUCTION

Guru Dutt was born in 1925 to a modest middle-class family. His father, who worked as an administrative clerk in Burmah Shell Company, had studied English literature and wrote poetry that remained unpublished. Guru Dutt's mother, who had a troubled relationship with her husband, had a great zest for life. Guru Dutt's brother, Atmaram, says: "We came from a lower middle-class family, so there was a lot of ambition to do well. Success was very important; it was very necessary to do things in life. My mother fired that ambition."

Although he travelled a lot with his mother to many cities — Bangalore, Mangalore, Madras, Ahmedabad — it was in Calcutta that the family lived together for a long time which happened to be Guru Dutt's growing years too. Bengal and its

Guru Dutt in *Baaz*

culture were to have a deep impact on Guru Dutt's life and work. He never went to college, but he was very well read – a trait he imbibed from his father. Atmaram remembers, "He spoke Hindi very well, but he was more at home in English and in Bengali. At home we spoke Konkani with a lot of English too. He thought in English and wrote in English and that's the truth." At 15, Guru Dutt, who had a flair for dancing, expressed his desire to his uncle, B. B. Benegal, a painter, to join Uday Shankar's dance troupe. He left a year later for Almora, to join Uday Shankar's India Culture Centre, without even collecting his salary of Rs 40 from his first job as a telephone operator at a mill.

When this Centre closed down due to lack of funds during the war, Guru Dutt returned home in 1944. His family was now in Bombay. Benegal introduced him to Baburao Pai, the Chief Executive of the Prabhat Film Company and Studio in Poona. Dutt was employed as a dance director at the studio on a three-year contract. He also started working as assistant director and as an actor in small roles. Dutt worked in Poona for two years. Here he met Dev Anand, who also worked at Prabhat; he also came to know Rehman. Pai later set up his own company in Bombay. Guru Dutt worked for him there till 1947, when his contract with Pai ended. He was out of work for many months, but eventually found work as assistant director to Amiya Chakravarty, Gyan Mukherjee and others. Dev Anand, keeping a promise he had made earlier, offered Dutt the opportunity to direct *Baazi* (1951) for Navketan, the company he had set up with his brother Chetan Anand. Dev Anand, already a star by then, played the lead role in this and the next film Guru Dutt directed — *Jaal* (1952).

It was during the making of *Baazi* that Guru Dutt met Geeta Roy, an established singer. They got married in 1953. In 1953 itself, Dutt set up his own production company called Guru Dutt Productions, which henceforth produced all his films. In 1952 he had set up a production company called H.G. Films with Haridarshan Kaur, who was actress

Geeta Bali's sister. This company produced only one film directed by Guru Dutt: *Baaz* (1953). It was the first film that Dutt was to star in, in the lead role. The story was set in the 16th century and the film did not do well at the box-office. *Aar Paar* (1954) was Guru Dutt Productions' first film, and it proved a hit. This was followed by *Mr and Mrs 55* (1955) and *CID* (1956), produced by Dutt and directed by his assistant, Raj Khosla. *Sailaab* (1956), produced by Geeta Dutt's brother, Mukul Roy and directed by Guru Dutt, did not create any ripples at the box-office. *Pyaasa* (1957), based on an early script written by Dutt, entitled *Kashmakash*, was the next film he directed. Its sombre mood was in stark contrast to the spirit of the two films that had preceded it, *Aar Paar* and *Mr and Mrs 55*. The film did well at the box-office and remains one of the high points of not only Guru Dutt's career, but also of the Hindi cinema.

The self-reflective *Kaagaz ke Phool* (1959), India's first film in cinemascope, followed; it too remains one of the landmark films in the history of Hindi cinema, but it flopped badly.

Guru Dutt did not recover from the rejection of the film by the audience and henceforth did not sign his name as director. *Chaudvin ka Chand* (1960) directed by M. Sadiq, produced by Dutt with himself in the lead role, was the biggest commercial success of Guru Dutt's company. *Sahib, Bibi aur Ghulam* (1962), directed by his long-time friend and dialogue writer, Abrar Alvi, was the last film which Dutt produced and acted in. The turmoil in his marriage, his troubled love-life, his alcoholism and his own lonely, troubled and intense nature contributed to the many attempts at suicide that he made. His death in 1964, at the age of 39 is widely believed to be a case of suicide.

As a director, Guru Dutt experimented with many genres: a historical (*Baaz*), thrillers (*Baazi, Jaal, Aar Paar*), a social comedy (*Mr and Mrs 55*), a social (*Pyaasa*), and a self-reflective film with autobiographical elements (*Kaagaz ke Phool*).

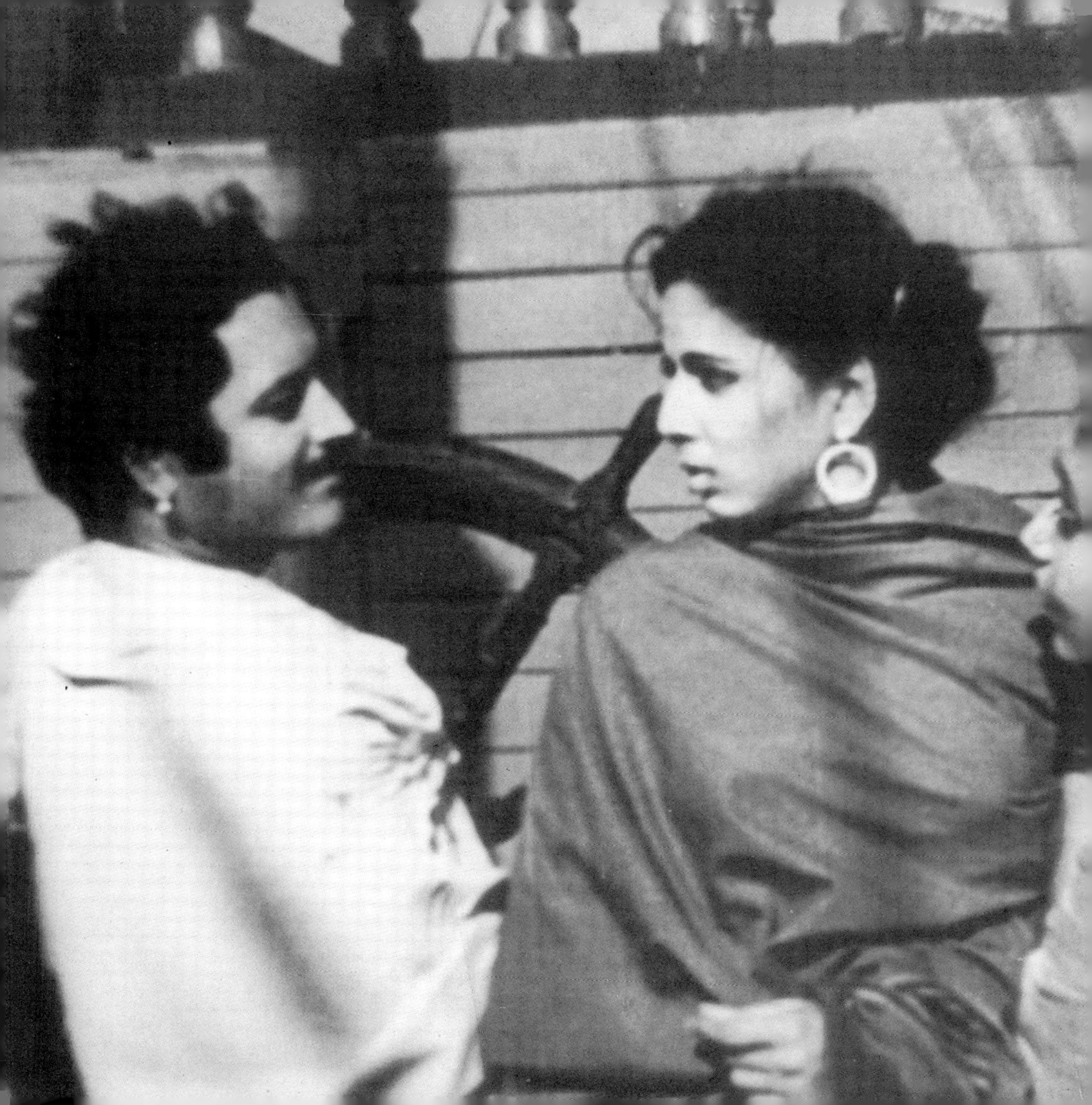

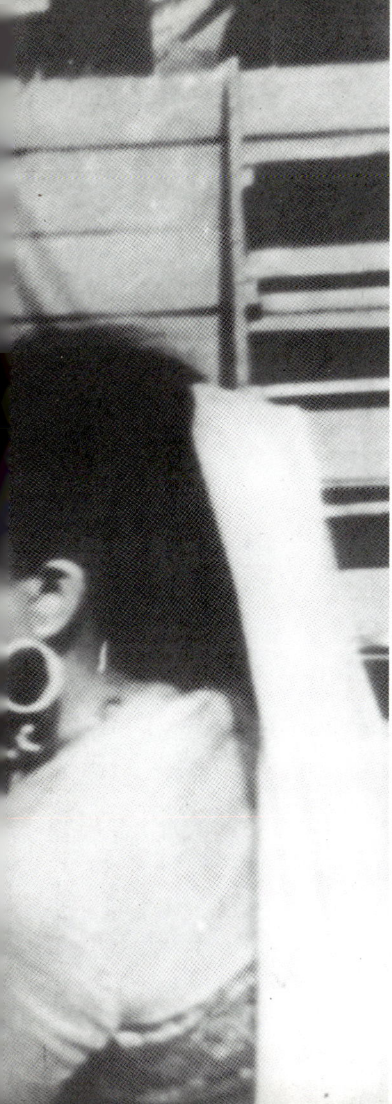

2

THE GOLDEN FIFTIES

The post-Independence period saw the emergence of many directors who crafted distinctive styles in their handling of the themes they had chosen to focus upon. Iqbal Masud, in his article, 'The Great Four of the Golden Fifties', is quick to point out that the worldview of directors who would be counted in the Golden Pantheon of the fifties — Mehboob Khan, Bimal Roy, Guru Dutt and Raj Kapoor — were formed in the traumatic years of the thirties and forties:

"The fight for Independence, famines,

Guru Dutt and Geeta Bali in *Baaz*

changing social mores, the global fight against fascism, all contributed to the ethos in which the directors grew up.

"There are many common traits in the works of these directors. The foremost is that much-abused word 'humanism'...It was fuelled by outrage against India's savage poverty and inequalities (exacerbated by the rise of the black market in the Second World War). A second element was its deep awareness of India's past and present cultures — both 'high' and 'popular'. A third was the skill in communicating its outrage and call for change to the masses. This last element has been called 'entertainment'. But in the forties and fifties this had an aspirational touch about it which had vanished long ago from our cinema."

Narratives about criminals — usually thieves — function as the 'limit-text' of an era. In times of transition and turmoil, it is characters who do not follow the rules of the system and who, by being on the threshold of the systemic and non-systemic, test the laws of the system. The play of centre and periphery, where the centre is the law of the system, and the periphery, the location where the character is situated, is very important in the narratives of the fifties. The resolution of conflict in fact, is the pulling of the peripheral protagonist into the orbit of the system, into the rule of institutions and their view of social justice. The 'heroes' of many of the fifties' films are actually 'anti-heroes' to the extent that that they do not, till the climatic moment of the narrative, follow the rules of the system. They are represented as 'heroes' precisely because they ultimately submit to the logic of the system. Raj Kapoor's *Awaara*, Vijay Anand's *Kala Bazaar*, Guru Dutt's *Baaz* and *Jaal* — all have criminals as their lead protagonists. Even Mehboob Khan in his *Mother India* (1957), although he deals with the countryside on an epic scale, has a Birju, who becomes a dacoit because he intuitively knows that the system cannot deliver the justice he wants for his mother.

The narratives of the Hindi cinema of the fifties are infused with an optimism and faith in post-colonial India. There is the

Gandhian belief in the equality of all religions, castes and classes and a Nehruvian belief in the ability of all institutions being set up in post-Independent India to dispense social justice. This welding of the visions of the Father of the Nation (Gandhi) and the Father of the Indian State (Nehru) found an articulation in the Hindi cinema of the fifties, contributing to what Masud calls the 'aspirational touch'. It was to give the narratives of the outlaw their specific character: they were 'thrillers' – but not in the Hollywoodian sense – for they were 'socials' too! What makes a criminal and what pushes people into criminal activity – these were some of the questions posed in the films of the fifties. If *Awaara* elaborated the theme that 'society, not genes, produces criminals', the films of Vijay Anand and Guru Dutt charted the social compulsions, the life of no exit in the lower depths. It is Guru Dutt who goes the farthest: in the character of Tony (actor Dev Anand) in *Jaal* he comes closest to creating a negative character who has absolutely no qualms about his life

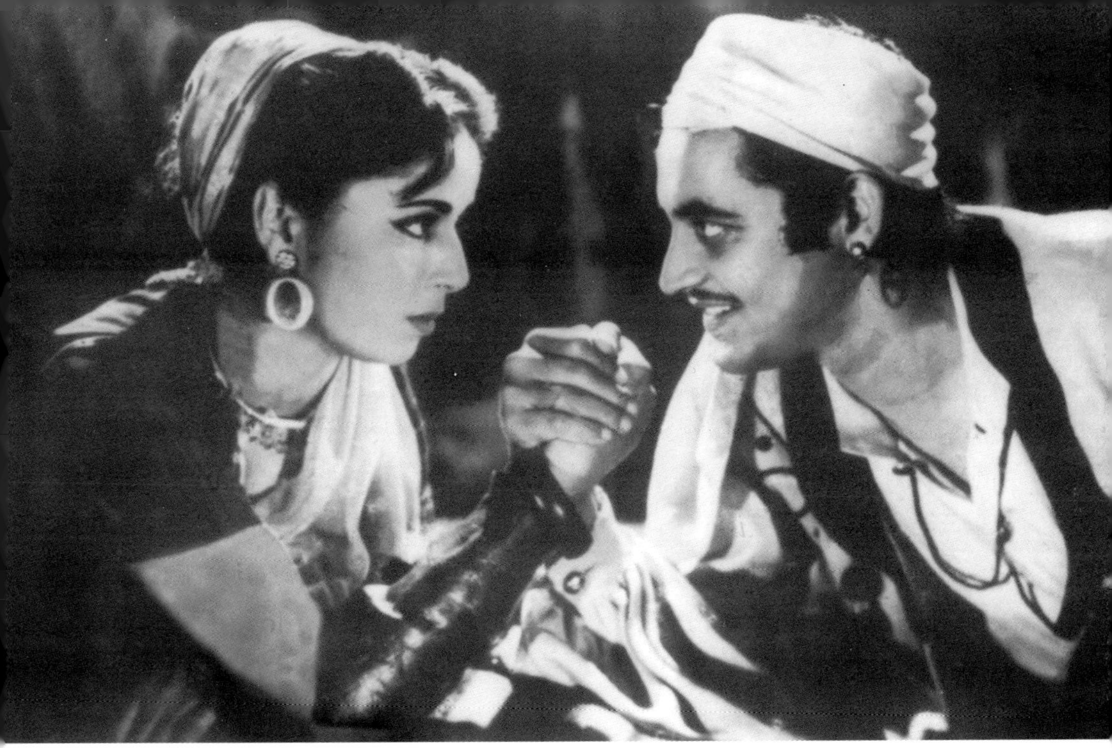

Geeta Bali with Guru Dutt in *Baaz*

as a criminal and as a person who leads trusting women, in love with him, astray. He seems to be innately 'bad', for there is no explanation given as to why he is what he is. In this, Tony seems to be sharing kinship bonds with the Hollywood noir-hero, a movement the social thriller of the fifties drew upon. While the lead male protagonist of *Jaal* shares a lot in common with the noir hero, the film itself is closer to the realism of post-war Italy. The plot unfolds among a community of fisherfolk in Goa and in the sequences where the community is shown fishing, or at sea, the film reminds one of Visconti's *La Terra Trema*. Atmaram, Guru Dutt's brother says that "*Jaal* was based to a large extent on *Bitter Rice*" (Guiseppe de Santis's 1948-Italian film, *Riso Amaro*).

The relationship of the social thriller to noir, in fact, provides an interesting study of the way in which movements journey to different lands and are adapted into and reinvented in different contexts. If German expressionism was an aesthetic coming to terms with the tumultuous times before and after the First World War, then noir, which drew on expressionism, expressed the angst of the crisis of values of the post-war generation. Hollywood made the aesthetics of noir known worldwide and this was imbibed and adapted to the

Indian context in the post-colonial period. The aesthetics of noir and expressionism – the negative characters, the dark and sombre mood, the preoccupation with the city and its mean streets, the femme fatale – all entered the Hindi cinema in the post-colonial period in order to represent the anxieties of the dispossessed, of the marginal characters and to reaffirm faith in the rule of the institutions of social justice. The movement of noir cinema was a repertoire that could be drawn upon stylistically, thematically, technically, and in terms of characterisation. *Awaara*, for instance, uses a complex, grainy and convoluted texture (of surroundings, ground, background, whether in the *chawl* where Raj lives, or in Nature, or in the houses of the rich) through the film to create the ambience or 'material equivalence' of Raj's tortured self. In the films of Guru Dutt, it is the streets that figure as a character in their own right. Where Guru Dutt differs from other film-makers in his portrayal of the criminal is that he is not overly preoccupied with the distinction between the rich and the poor and the corresponding division of the city space (as in Raj Kapoor's *Awaara* and *Shri 420*). Guru Dutt's characters are creatures of the street and are at home on the street: Kalu in *Aar Paar*, Tony in *Jaal* and Vijay in *Pyaasa* are never seen properly 'housed'. Guru Dutt's works, in fact, posit what I would like to call the 'narrative of homelessness'. The characters are 'outsiders' in an additional sense: they are 'outsiders' because they may have returned after a stint in jail (Kalu in *Aar Paar*), or because they have come to Goa from the big city of Bombay (Tony in *Jaal*), or because they have been rejected by philistines (Vijay in *Pyaasa*); they are also 'outsiders' because they have no space they can relate to as 'home'. This is also true of Suresh Sinha in *Kaagaz ke Phool*, who, though a celebrated and wealthy filmmaker, has his home life in shambles.

The social circumstances that pushed an individual into crime were meticulously dealt with by Raj Kapoor, Vijay Anand and Guru Dutt, but in different ways. In the Navketan films (*Baazi*, directed by Guru Dutt and *Kala Bazaar* in 1960,

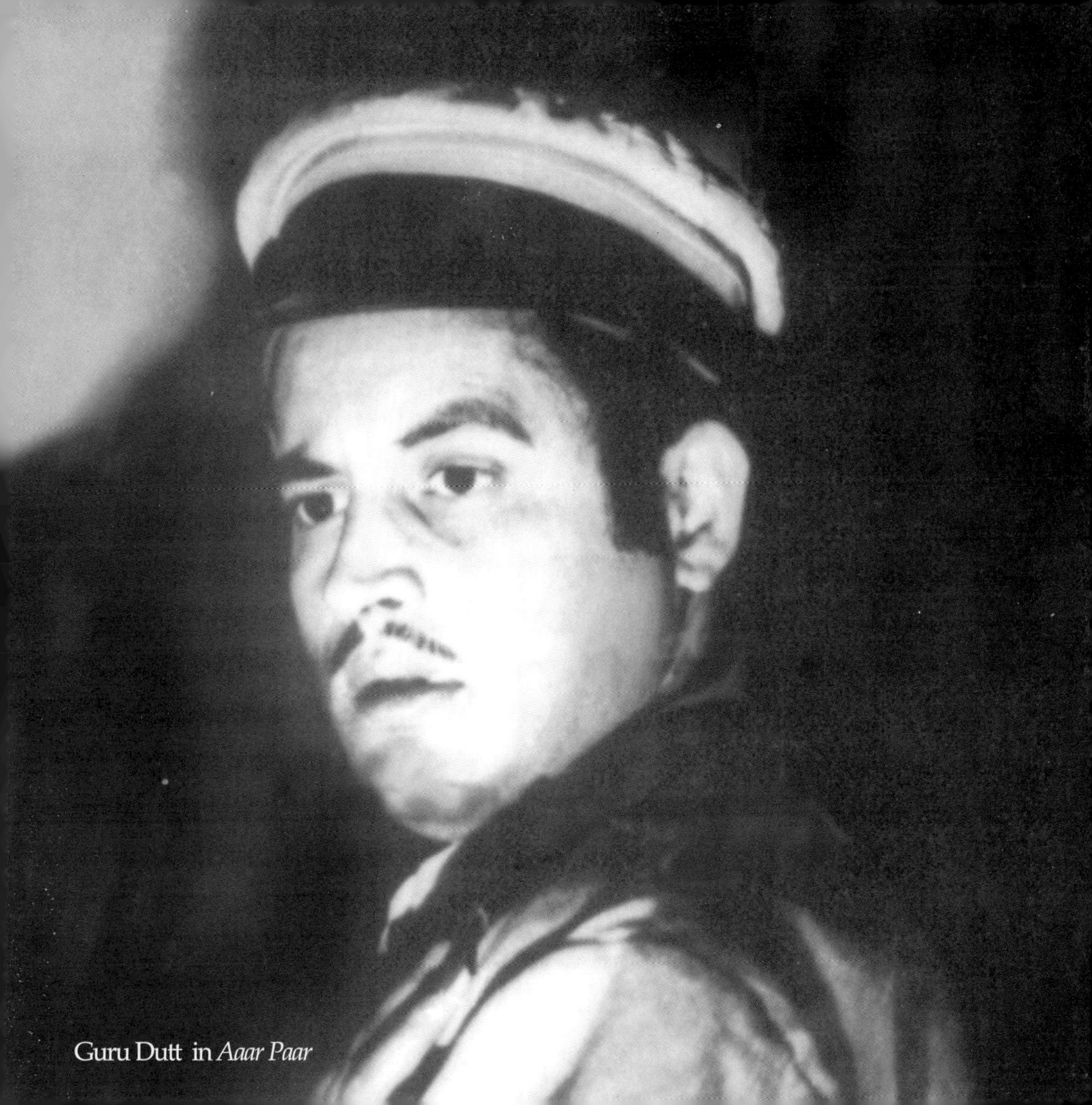

Guru Dutt in *Aaar Paar*

directed by Vijay Anand), the effort is to achieve a greater sense of realism, a grimmer feel of the lower depths. If Raj Kapoor presents the narrative as an individual's descent into crime and inscribes his narrative in a debate about criminality being engendered by social and not genetic factors, the Navketan films make the condition more universal and more modern. This is done through several narrative markers. One of the important differences between the two worldviews is in the representation of the street. Raj Kapoor singing '*Awaara hoon...*' shows streets that are also benign: women who playfully throw him off the truck, children playing on the street. The streets in *Baazi*, directed by Guru Dutt for Navketan and made in the same year as *Awaara* (1951), are not so benign. The very first shot of the film shows Pedro get off a car, to scout for a small-time gambler in the casino he works for. He walks by another man sitting on a kerb, goes into a narrow gully, and talks to the woman at the door of a building. Inside, men are gambling. It is Madan (Dev Anand) who has the magic hand that throws a six on the dice every time. The sense of the underbelly of the city (of big-time and petty gamblers) is established in this opening sequence without any explanations. The lame girl, who kisses his hand and seems to bring the hero luck, is an incidental character, but an important one, establishing that there are others apart from the hero and his family who are suffering the same social fate. Madan is forced to work for the don who owns the casino as he finds out that he has to provide medical treatment for his sister, who is suffering from tuberculosis. This Madan, however, is not filled with the burning sense of humiliation and mortification that Raj is filled with in *Awaara* (as in the scene where he slaps Nargis in *Awaara*), or a kind of self-pity (as in the scene where, completely dejected, Raj Kapoor finds companionship in a dog that comes up to him under the lamp-post; the pathos of the sequence is heavily underlined because the titles of the film have this very scene as the background).

Raj Kapoor was also preoccupied in the fifties with the

rich-poor divide in the cities and through *Awaara* charts with care the different streets inhabited by those with money and those without. Madan in *Baazi* is not sentimental; he is street smart and knows the cruelty of this world only too well. The sequence where he enters the casino to work for the first time is an example of this. The scene is tightly held together in a masterly way by the exchange of looks between the people present and the strumming of Nina's (actress Geeta Bali's) guitar. Madan realises bitterly that the manager would spend wads of notes for gambling in the casino, but would not tolerate a poor cleaner surreptitiously pick up a note that has fallen down. Raj Kapoor is interested in the genesis of the conflict between evil and good; Guru Dutt, on the other hand, never loses sight of the social canvas of cruelty, but deals with it in a more matter-of-fact way.

Guru Dutt's work also differs from the work of other directors of the Golden Pantheon of the fifties in what Masud has called his 'poetry of defeat'. *Pyaasa* marks the break from

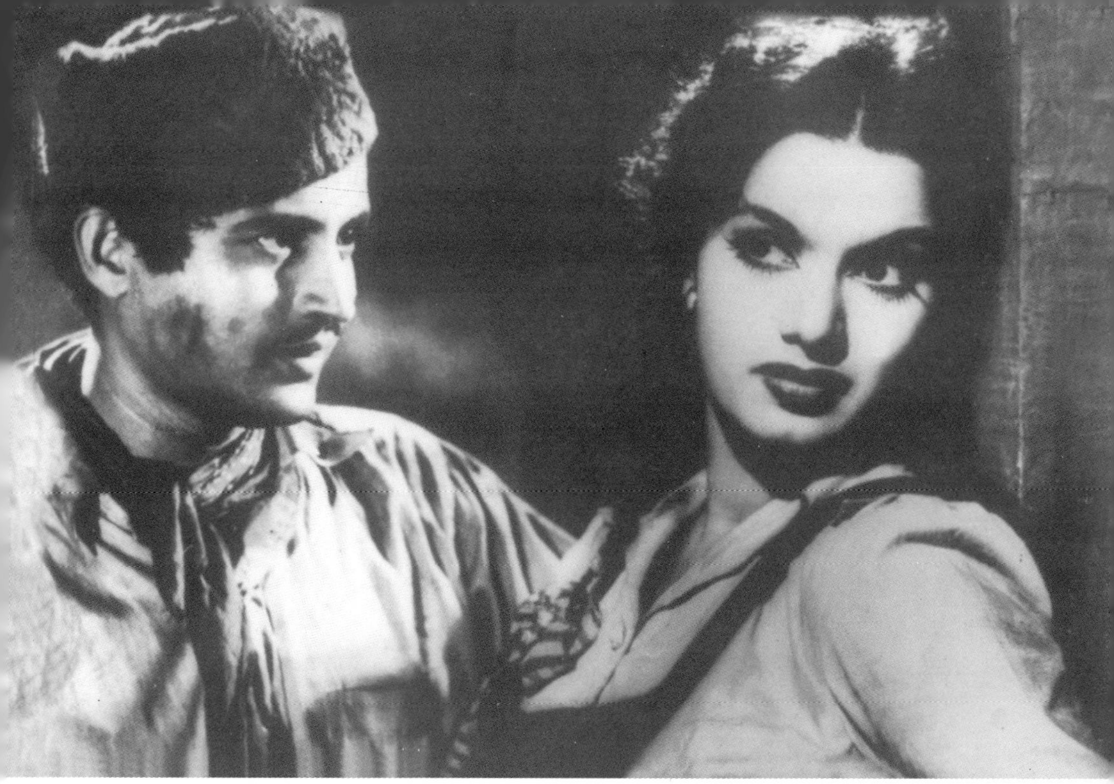

Guru Dutt with Shyama in *Aaar Paar*

his earlier works in precisely this tone of defeat. Whether the protagonist is someone who gives in to crime (Madan in *Baazi*), or is innately selfish and an outlaw (Tony in *Jaal*), or someone who moves in the world of crime, or gets indirectly involved in its activities but remains untainted by it (Kalu Birju in *Aar Paar*), there is hope for the reformation of his character. *Pyaasa* shifts the onus of reformation on to the society which is shown as incapable of reform. It is in this 'inverse narrative' that Guru Dutt's innovation lies; it is here that the pulse of his critique of post-Independence India is felt. This narrativisation of the individual's struggle against social forces that are too large, too hostile, too ridden with a corrupted or decadent sense of power, is the hallmark of Dutt's work from *Pyaasa* onwards. None of the other directors of the fifties and sixties dared to walk this path – it was too critical of the social milieu for one; it was too full of despair, for another.

In Guru Dutt's work (*Pyaasa* and *Kaagaz ke Phool*) we find the first articulations of a citizen who cannot be drawn into the system, through the character of the artiste as an outsider to a society whose norms he does not wish to conform to, and a society that is equally deaf to his creativity. While this is no doubt imbued with a romantic notion of the artist's self in opposition to the world, there is also the delineation of a broader social vision. It is in this very specific narrative of the individual pitted against social forces that overwhelm him/her, that *Sahib, Bibi aur Ghulam* also 'fits' into Guru Dutt's oeuvre. Thematically (and not just stylistically) *Sahib, Bibi aur Ghulam* further explores and renders more complex the theme of the 'outsider'.

The fifties saw the 'solidification' and entrenchment of many genres in the Hindi cinema in the post-colonial context. While most of the leading directors of the time worked with many kinds of plots and contributed to their 'moulding and setting', it was Guru Dutt alone who created the narrative of a character who remained non-systemic and averse to the pull of the centre.

Contributing to the 'golden lustre' of the 'Golden Fifties' were the progressive writers, actors, music directors, dancers who were associated in diverse ways with the progressive

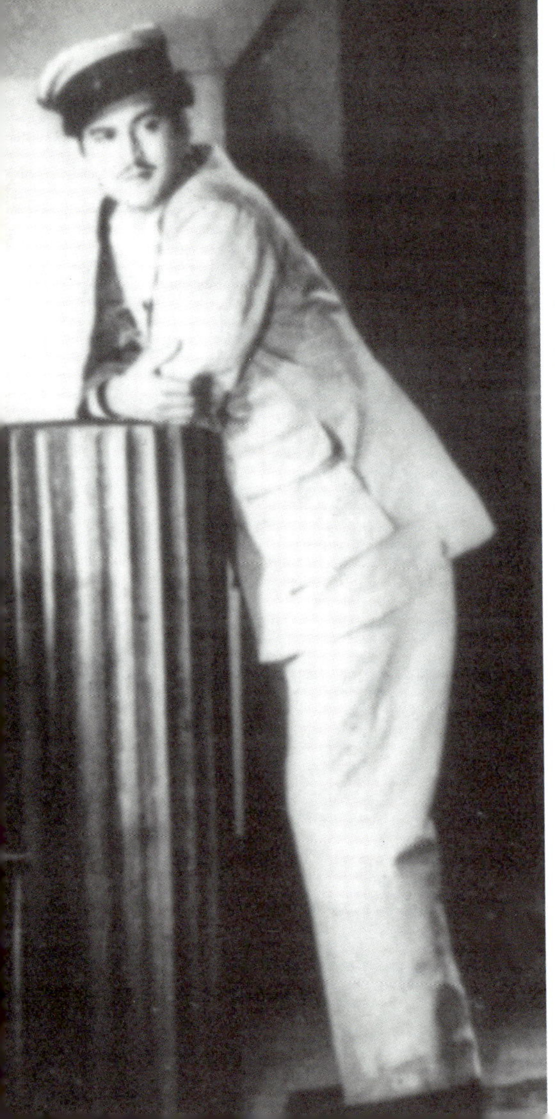

Indian Peoples Theatre Association (IPTA). K. A. Abbas, Salil Chowdhary, Sahir Ludhianvi, Balraj Sahni, Kaifi Azmi, to name a few, were to colour the worldview expressed in songs, scripts, characterisation and music. If the storylines on criminals were drawing on noir narratives and aesthetics to present the world of the criminal, the IPTA vision of social critique, struggle and social change, if not revolution, also infused the narratives. The Hindi film-text could thus be seen

Guru Dutt in *Aaar Paar*

as a matrix with several nodal points, each node often exhibiting a different pressure point vis-à-vis the protagonist and notions of social justice – one point could express a faith in the Nehruvian vision in institutions that were coming into being to dispense social justice, another could express hopelessness and defeat, while yet another could call for an active struggle for social transformation. These differently nuanced pressure points, however, did not usually hinder the representation of an overarching vision that the work conveyed. Masud astutely points out that *Pyaasa*, in fact, was an amalgamation of three differing views. The dialogue writer, Abrar Alvi, was fascinated by the artist-society girl-prostitute love triangle. The lyricist Sahir Ludhianvi had a different outlook:

"Then came Sahir with his '*Yeh mahalon, yeh takhton, yeh taajon ki duniya…*' (What is it worth, this world of thrones and crowns…) raising the banner of revolution which simply confounded Alvi. At the Festival of Three Continents at

Nantes, I was closely questioned about this 'merger' by French critics — 'Isn't it self-indulgence to fuse personal disappointment in love with establishment hatred?'

"Absolutely right. But here a third element entered. What is crudely called Dutt's 'death wish' and which I call his 'poetry of defeat'— Dutt was strongly possessed by death, but this was a lyrical attachment to grace in defeat..."

If the fifties was a period of the 'settling down' of generic forms in the cinema, it was also a period of the formation of very distinctive styles in the Hindi cinema. Since directors usually worked with the same teams (actors, technicians, lyricists, music directors) over a period of time, they were able to work out their styles in putting scenes 'on stage'. Raj Kapoor had his preferred lyricists, music directors and his cameraman Radhu Karmakar. Cameraman Faredoon Irani shot most of Mehboob's films. Guru Dutt worked with V.K Murthy— his cameraman in all his films, except *Baazi* (in which he was assistant cameraman) and *Chaudhvin ka Chand*; S. Guruswamy was his production controller from *Jaal* onwards; editor Y. G. Chawhan worked on all his films except *Jaal*. Art director Biren Naug, lyricists Sahir Ludhianvi, Majrooh Sultanpuri and Shakeel Badayuni, music composers O.P. Nayyar and S.D. Burman and the actors Geeta Bali, Waheeda Rehman, Johnny Walker, Dev Anand and Rehman worked with Dutt on several of his productions. This facilitated the creation of a distinctive style that bore Guru Dutt's signature. Nasreen Munni Kabir in *Guru Dutt: A Life in Cinema* writes, "Fluid camera movements, long tracking shots, brilliant use of close-ups, play of light and shade, intelligent dialogue, unpredictable plots, fine use of music, naturalistic performances and a psychological depth to his characters are the hallmarks of Guru Dutt's work."

Most of the directors of the fifties had also been schooled in the studio system and learnt their craft on the job. Dutt had worked at Prabhat Studios and assisted some of the important filmmakers of the time. The directors of the fifties were able to establish distinctive styles not only because they tended to work with the same teams over a period of time, but also because they were involved with more than one aspect of film-making: Raj Kapoor, like Guru Dutt, was actor/director/producer and in addition, he owned a studio; Mehboob was director/producer and owned a studio; Bimal Roy was cinematographer/director. These directors were also actively involved in scripting and in the music that was composed for their films. The multiple roles donned by the filmmakers contributed in no small way to the evolution and crafting of personal styles even as generic narratives came to be the mainstay of Hindi cinema. V.K. Murthy, in an interview, gives an indication of how closely the mise en scene of a Dutt film was linked to the vision of the director: "On the day he died, I was in Bangalore. The moment I got the telephone call, I was completely down in my mood… After some time, maybe you can call it selfishness, I thought I had lost a good person, and also my technique. That's exactly what happened. He had a jeweller's eye. Just as a jeweller can find out which is the best diamond, he had the knack of extracting the best from a person. That's how he has been very successful in having a good team of actors, technicians, music directors and art directors. He had that knack."

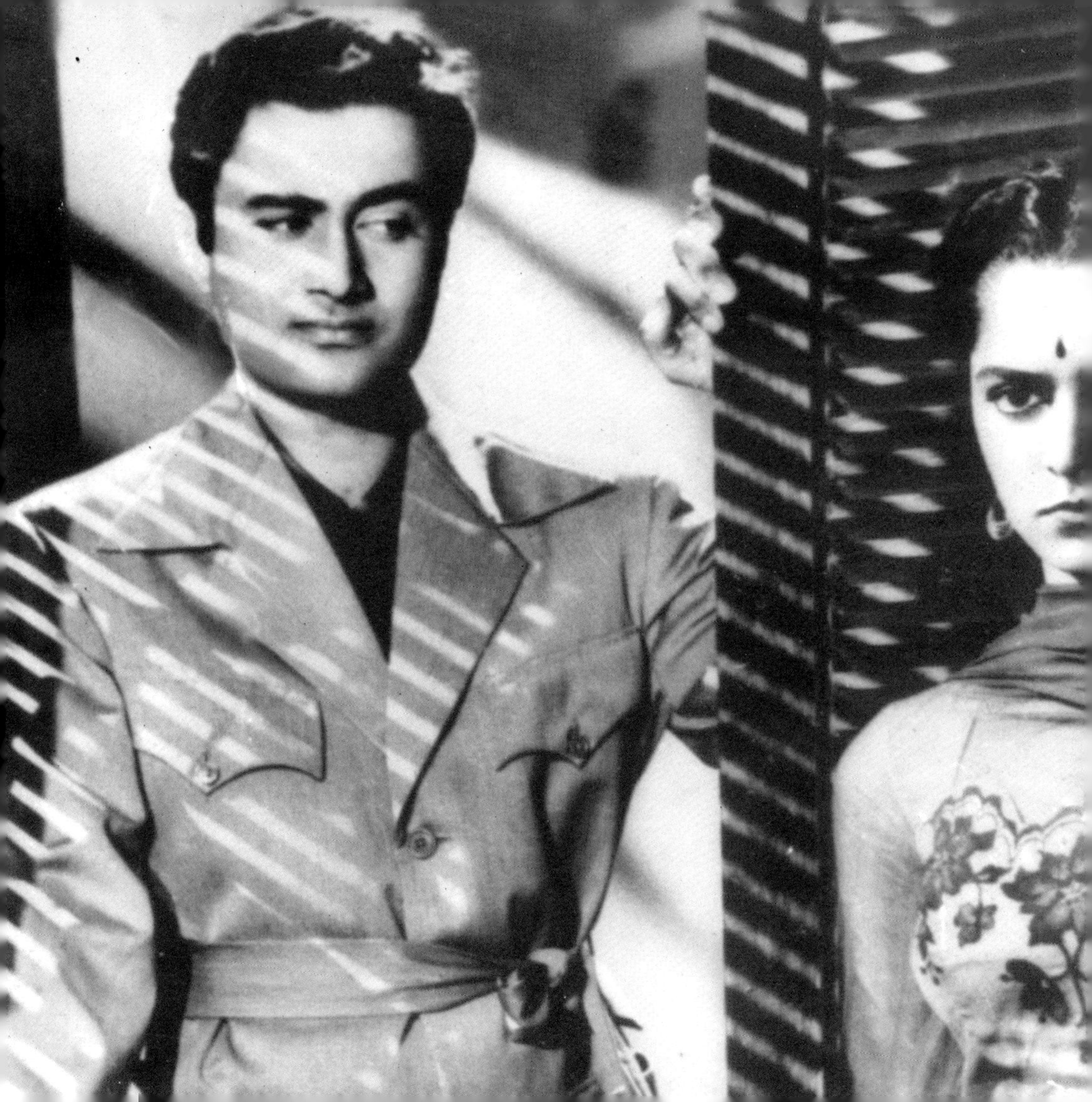

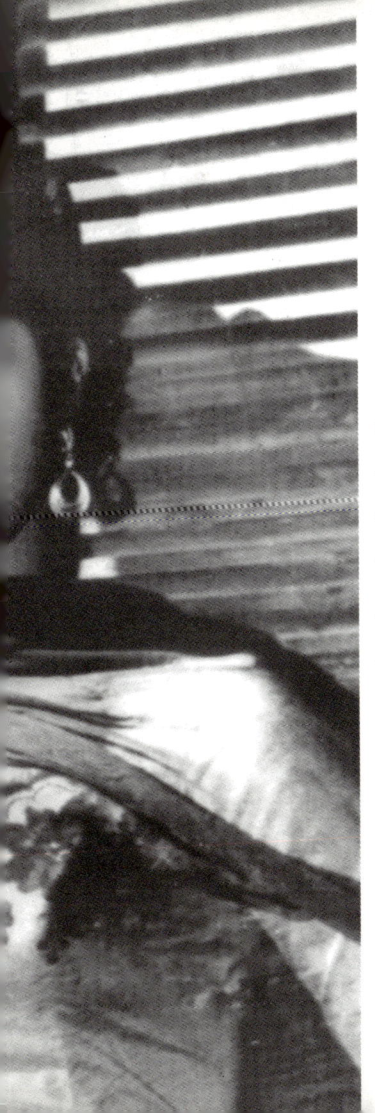

3

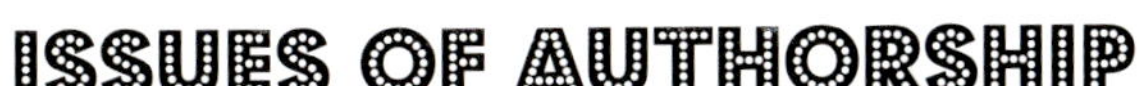

ISSUES OF AUTHORSHIP

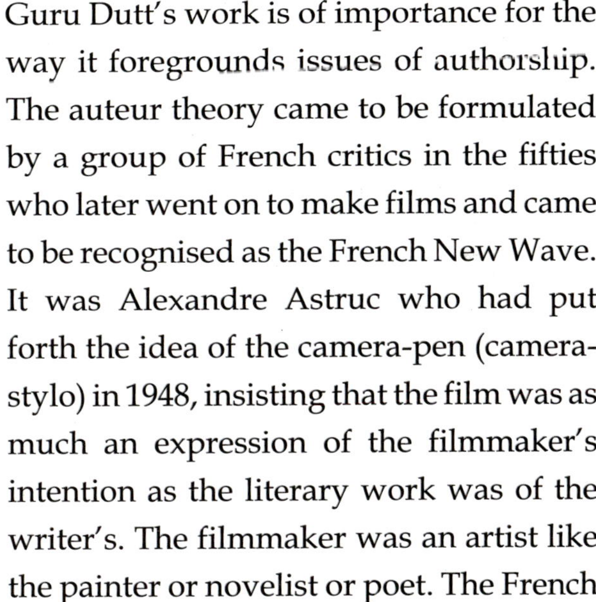

Guru Dutt's work is of importance for the way it foregrounds issues of authorship. The auteur theory came to be formulated by a group of French critics in the fifties who later went on to make films and came to be recognised as the French New Wave. It was Alexandre Astruc who had put forth the idea of the camera-pen (camera-stylo) in 1948, insisting that the film was as much an expression of the filmmaker's intention as the literary work was of the writer's. The filmmaker was an artist like the painter or novelist or poet. The French

Dev Anand and Waheeda Rehman in *CID*

critics of the fifties, particularly those working at the *Cahiers du Cinema*, moved away from the romantic underpinnings of this notion and argued in the context of the American films that fascinated them, that despite the tight grip on production that Hollywood as an industry exercised on filmmakers, some directors left their personal stamp on the films they made. This 'signature' of the auteur, the French critics stated, was to be seen in the way the filmmaker staged the scene, in the mise en scene. The focus was, therefore, not on the artist as the sole 'origin' of the film's meaning, but on the devices and techniques the filmmaker used to realise the cluster of themes he was dealing with. According to Fereydoun Hoveyda:

"The originality of an auteur lies not in the subject matter he chooses but in the technique he employs, in the mise en scene, through which everything is expressed on the screen....

"As Sartre said, 'One is not a writer because one has chosen to say certain things, but because one has chosen to say them in a certain way.' Why should it be different in our art? ...

What counts in a film is the striving towards order, harmony, composition; the placing of the actors and objects; the movements within the frame; the capture of a movement or look; in short, the intellectual operation which has set to work an initial emotion and a general idea. Mise en scene is nothing other than the technique which each auteur invents in order to express himself and establish the specificity of his work."

In the seventies, the auteur theory developed in the UK and USA created its own linkages with the reigning critical movements of structuralism, post-structuralism and post-modernism. Whatever the mutations of earlier positions, the auteur theory did bring the text into focus not only as a manifestation of a genre but as bearing the imprint of the film-maker in its mise en scene. Andre Bazin, reviewing and critiquing the '*politiques des auteurs*' in 1957, says: "Jacques Rivette has said that an auteur is someone who speaks in the first person. It's a good definition; let's adopt it."

Guru Dutt, as filmmaker, certainly spoke in the first

person in more ways than one. While working with the genre of the thriller, he charted his distinctive imagic style and thematic preoccupations. *Pyaasa* marks a break from Dutt's engagement with the social thriller as director and producer. (*CID*, produced by Dutt and directed by Raj Khosla, was also a thriller.) From *Pyaasa* onwards, he gave up the security of the genric mode to take up fictional biographies: of a poet, of a filmmaker, of a woman caught in the crumbling of a decadent social order. He strode the path of a near-autobiographical mode in *Kaagaz ke Phool*. In the last three films – *Pyaasa, Kaagaz ke Phool* and *Sahib, Bibi aur Ghulam*, Dutt grounds himself in a

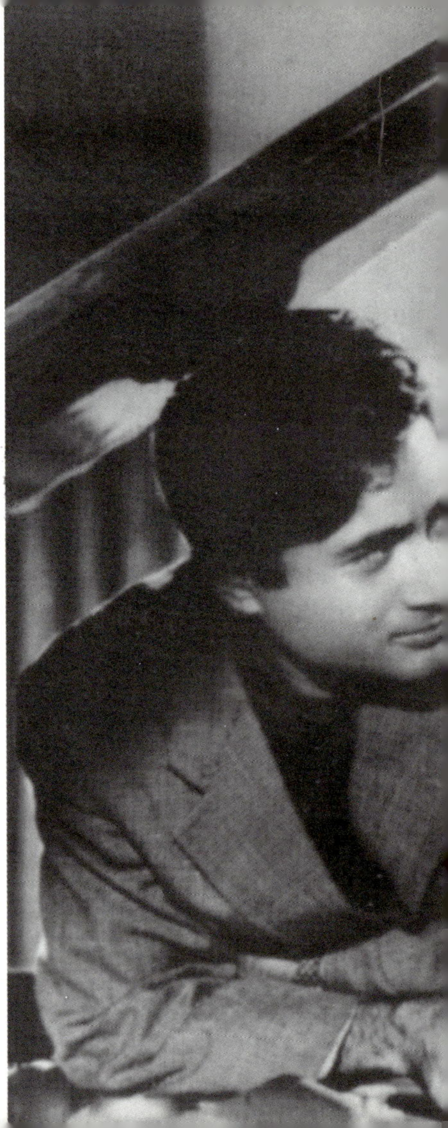

Dev Anand with Waheeda Rehman in *CID*

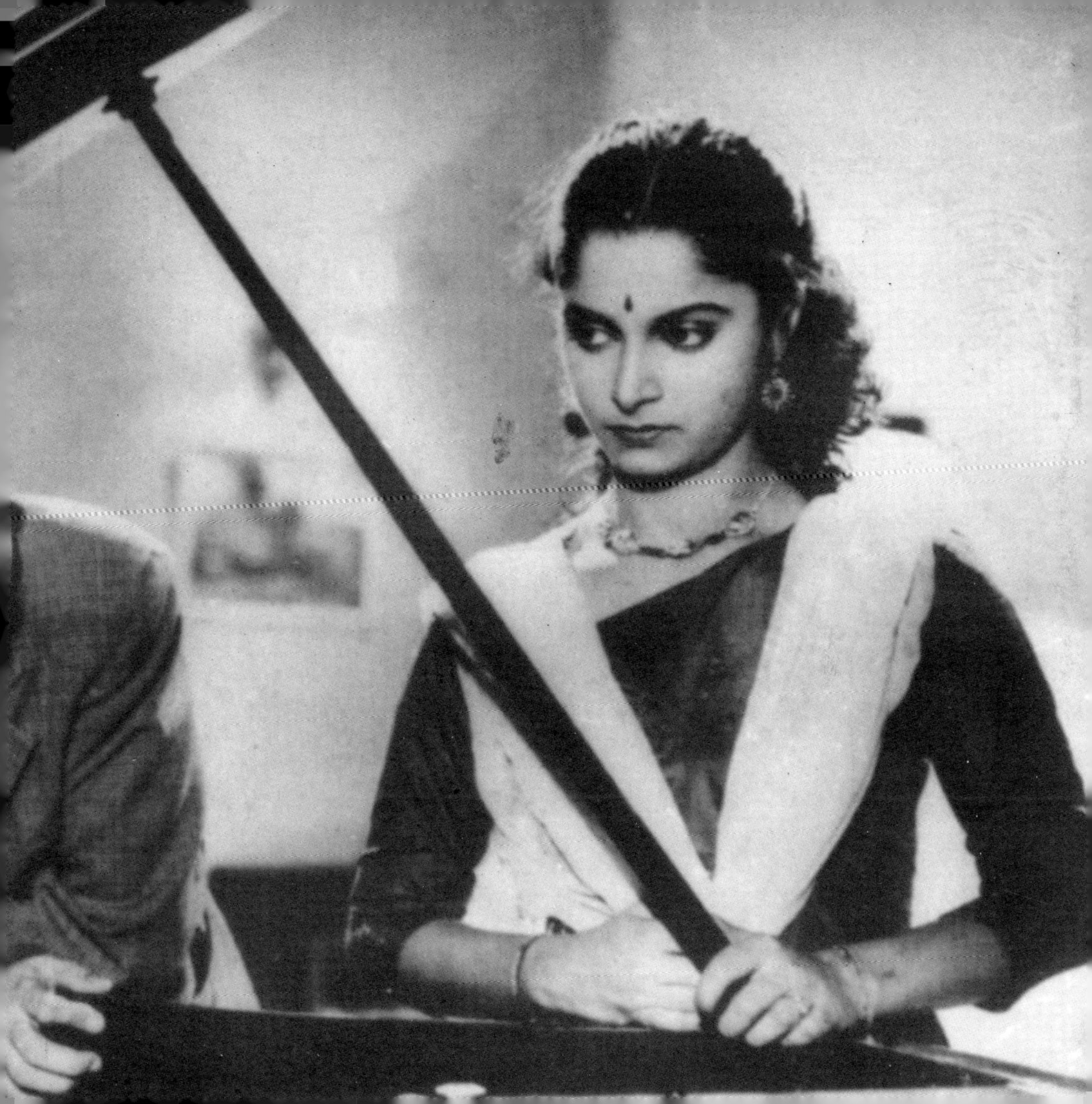

greater social realism, combined with, as Arun Khopkar has pointed out, the traditions of melodrama:

"Two outstanding Indian filmmakers in whose work the confessional element plays a vital part are Ritwik Ghatak and Guru Dutt...

"Firstly, both used melodrama as their basic form...

"Secondly, both artistes made the melodic aspect of melodrama an integral part of their work...They demonstrated that cinema was not a medium meant exclusively to reflect reality or communicate a 'message'. It was a medium that imposed its own rhythmic patterns of expression."

Social realism is expressed above all in Dutt's films in the disgust with growing commercialisation and the prevalence of hypocritical social mores which trample upon the dignity of the individual. Guru Dutt also broke with the existing codes of the industry, by having the films after *Pyaasa* end on a non-optimistic note. Even though *Pyaasa, Kaagaz ke Phool* and *Sahib, Bibi aur Ghulam* are fictional biographies, charting the journey of the protagonist from adulthood to death (real in *Kaagaz ke Phool* and *Sahib, Bibi aur Ghulam* and metaphorical in *Pyaasa*), they move beyond the personal tragedies of the protagonist to show the inexorable, suffocating logic of a larger social reality. Guru Dutt created a personal style within the framework of genre cinema (working predominantly with the thriller) and then moved on to create the narrative framework for a romantic-realist social melodrama within the Hindi film industry. This in itself was a radical step. Guru Dutt forged a distinctive style that ran through his work, through all its phases. Dutt is an auteur for being preoccupied with 'how' the subject matter was to be conveyed; he is also an auteur for formulating a new subject matter. The irony of Dutt's life and work, had he himself realised it, was not that *Kaagaz ke Phool* flopped, but that sombre films such as *Pyaasa* and *Sahib, Bibi aur Ghulam* did well at all!

Guru Dutt was an artiste who spoke in the first person in

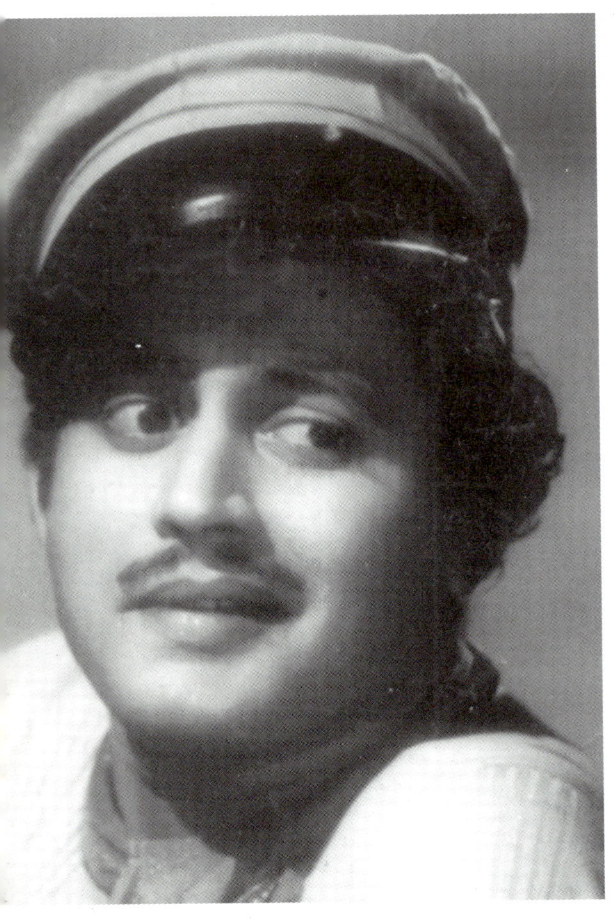

Guru Dutt in *Aaar Paar*

another way: he was also the lead actor in the films he produced and directed from *Baaz* onwards. He created a persona that was as important as the triad of Raj Kapoor, Dev Anand and Dilip Kumar. While the contribution of this triad to the creation of three distinct energies in post-Independence India has received critical attention, the persona of Guru Dutt as an actor in his own films has not been placed on the same plane, even though it deserves to be there. With Guru Dutt we have a thinking, urbane hero, unlike the other three. Raj Kapoor in his films of the fifties developed the persona of the simpleton tramp; Dev Anand was urbane and moved with a lightness of being; Dilip Kumar was the opposite – he cultivated an intense and 'weighty' presence that made itself felt predominantly through the grain of his voice. Guru Dutt, in contrast, cultivated the persona of the misunderstood man: but unlike Dilip Kumar, even in his tragic roles, his presence was not weighty; not sonorous. Unlike Dev Anand, his lightness of being was a thinking one; and unlike Raj Kapoor, his worldview was more politically incisive. This made the Dutt persona more sceptical and cynical.

While *Kaagaz ke Phool* is the last film he signed with his own name, it is widely believed that *Sahib, Bibi aur Ghulam* was also his film. Some include *Chaudhvin ka Chand* as well in Guru Dutt's directorial filmography, but because it was set in the Muslim milieu, it is more readily accepted that it was directed by M. Sadiq. According to Nasreen Munni Kabir, "Guru Dutt ignored the advice of colleagues who believed that M. Sadiq's career was over. He entrusted Sadiq with the direction of the film, but picturised the songs himself." Kabir also writes that according to Abrar Alvi, Guru Dutt only directed the songs and not the whole of *Sahib, Bibi aur Ghulam*.

Since the picturisation of songs is considered to be one of the hallmarks of Guru Dutt's style, and songs play a very important part of the narrative in these films, Guru Dutt can anyway be considered a co-director of both the films. While *Chaudhvin ka Chand* enters less into the debate of authorship, *Sahib, Bibi aur Ghulam* is a more complex case for several reasons. This film, in a very specific sense, continues with the preoccupations of *Pyaasa* and *Kaagaz ke Phool*. It also continues with an earlier fascination in Guru Dutt for socio-historical settings, as in *Jaal* and *Baaz*. Guru Dutt was committed to the portrayal of strong women characters. If most of the films made till *Pyaasa* exhibit a strong feel for the genre of the thriller, from *Pyaasa* onwards he veers towards the social melodrama. Through both the periods of his work, he remained steadfast to the creation of women characters, who, even when he was drawing on stereotypes (such as the femme fatale of noir, as expressed in the characters of Geeta Bali and Shakila in *Baaz* and *Aar Paar* respectively), were imbued with a strong sense of individuality. *Sahib, Bibi aur Ghulam* is a social melodrama and it is difficult to believe that a director for a first film within the industry, would choose to direct a non-genre film. This film also depicts women characters who are out of the ordinary. *Aar Paar, Pyaasa* and *Kaagaz ke Phool* explore homelessness. *Sahib, Bibi aur Ghulam* explores 'dehoming'. What is of added interest here is that the dehoming is explored in the context of Choti Bahu — one of the two lead women characters of the film. There is also a structural opposition, a 'master antinomy', running through the trilogy — the individual taking a stand against the hypocritical social mores of the time, and of not conforming. Vijay in *Pyaasa* refuses to accept the 'favours' of a society that would rather see him dead; Sinha in *Kaagaz ke Phool* refuses to go back to a studio that threw him out as soon he failed to deliver a hit, discounting all the profit he had brought in with his films; Choti Bahu in *Sahib, Bibi aur Ghulam* refuses to accept the secondary role she has to play to the nautch girls her husband spends all his time with. Other hallmarks of Dutt's style of filmmaking, seen through the body of his work till *Kaagaz ke Phool*, are also present in *Sahib, Bibi aur Ghulam*. All this contributes to making a strong case for attributing the direction of the film to Guru Dutt.

Guru Dutt's work poses many other questions vis-à-vis the theory of authorship. If the auteur is the artist whose intention infuses the material, then mise en scene is that collective effort that realises the narrative. The auteur-mise en scene couple paradoxically brings together the dynamics of the individual and the collective. The tension inherent between the notions of the auteur and of mise en scene was noted by Bazin. In his 1957 article, Bazin points out that "the

American cinema is a classical art, but why not then admire in it what is most admirable, i.e. not only the talent of this or that filmmaker, but the genius of the system, the richness of its ever-vigorous tradition, and its fertility when it comes into contact with new elements…" Bazin also notes that an auteur may make a mediocre film, while a mediocre director may turn out a good film. The director as sole author of the American film has been actively questioned. According to Stephen Crofts: "Cases have been made for the producer as author (e.g. Val Lewton, Arthur Freed), performer as author (e.g. the Marx brothers, Clint Eastwood as actor, Mae West), and scriptwriter as author (e.g. Jules Furthman, Ben Hecht, Frank Nugent). It is from the scriptwriter's viewpoint that directorial auteurism has been most forcefully debated. Richard Corliss argues for a *politique des collaborateurs*, that "scripts have to be considered alongside, if not before, direction…"

That mise en scene calls for a *politique des collaborateurs* is no doubt true, but it is not just the script-writer whose contribution has to be focused on. In Dutt's work, if the individual found triple inscriptions within and without the film (as producer, director and actor), then in the mise en scene, in the collective effort, too, his stamp was palpable. V.K. Murthy has said that when he heard Dutt had died, he felt that his own technique, too, had passed on. This statement can be read as an emotional tribute to a filmmaker, but it is also an interesting pointer to the fact that a specific kind of camera-work, with its density and complexity, could only be realised in a given context. Murthy, in an interview with director/cameraman Govind Nihalani, says: "Guru Dutt was the person who pushed me to do anything I wanted. He wouldn't stop me from doing whatever I wanted to do. That's the main thing. If a person wants to do some creative work, but he doesn't have support from the main people, the opportunity, and the equipment, then he can't create. Therefore, don't give me the credit. That credit should go to the persons who have encouraged me, and given me the equipment I wanted."

Dutt's work epitomises, on the one hand, the romantic extreme of the artiste as an individual whose signature is recognisable in every film he directs, in the genric and non-genric mode; on the other hand, Dutt's work, more than that of any other contemporary director, also exhibits the opposite tendency: one may speak of the stamp of his style in the works of other directors whose films were produced by him. Guru Dutt was an auteur not only as a director,

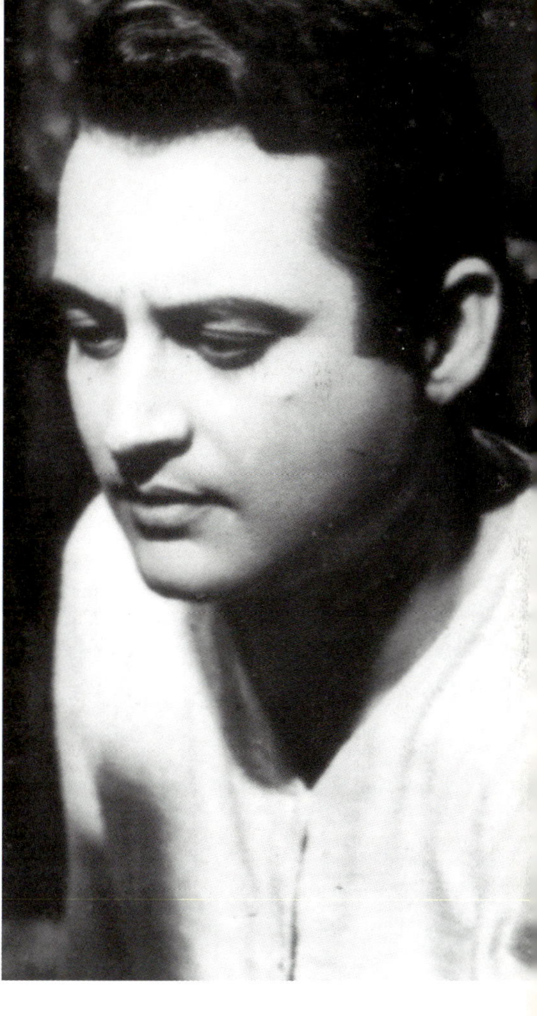

Guru Dutt in *Sahib, Bibi aur Ghulam*

but as a producer too. This is more than a case of 'influence'. Raj Khosla's *CID*, produced by Guru Dutt, exhibits many of the markers of Guru Dutt's style, particularly in the use of noir elements and in the song-picturisations. The question of who 'directed' *CID*, however, never arose. This was probably because Raj Khosla went on to direct many films and came to be acknowledged as a director in his own right with many hits to his credit. (Abrar Alvi, on the contrary, did not direct any film after *Sahib, Bibi aur Ghulam* although he was writing dialogues and screenplays for Hindi films into the nineties.) Or again, because Guru Dutt didn't act in *CID*, he was not seen as intervening in the film. (Dutt played the lead roles in both *Chaudhvin ka Chand* and *Sahib, Bibi aur Ghulam*.) The acts of production and acting were as much 'author-functions' for Dutt as direction.

If we examine the films that Dutt produced, we find specific motifs running through them, irrespective of whether Dutt directed them or not. Their repeated appearance in Dutt's work, however, points to his 'attachment' to these motifs: their differing treatments in the films further emphasise the thematic significance they wielded. A recurring motif in his films was that of the coat which, when it changes hands, bonds the protagonists to each other: in *Aar Paar*, Kalu Birju accuses Niki (actress Shyama) of having stolen his coat with money in it; in *Kaagaz ke Phool*, director Suresh Sinha meets Shanti for the first time in pouring rain – he gives her his coat and she comes to his studio in Bombay to return it; Inspector Shekhar gives it to a shivering Rekha in the car on a rainy night in Khosla's *CID*. It is in *Pyaasa*, however, that the coat is given far greater thematic embedding. Completely dejected by the rejection of his former lover and her publisher-husband and by the death of his mother, Vijay, in a drunken state, repeatedly asks Gulab why he should live at all. The next day, sober, but still in a dark mood, Vijay wanders on the station. He gives away his coat to an old and haggard beggar.

The beggar follows him; his foot gets caught in the tracks

and he is crushed to death by a train. The sequence is almost Dostoevskian in its conception of the 'double'. The beggar functions as an inverse double for Vijay in his physical and mental state of mind, in much the same way as Rogozhin does for Myshkin in *The Idiot*. The beggar follows Vijay as if pulled by a magnet through the dark alleys in the station. Vijay realises that he is being followed and hides. The beggar follows him nonetheless. When the beggar's leg gets caught, Vijay tries to pull him out of it. In a final gesture, the beggar pushes his benefactor away. Vijay survives; his identity, tied to his coat, is dead. There is an inexorable intertwining of two fates. Was Vijay anyway contemplating suicide? Does the beggar follow him because he has seen the death-wish in Vijay's eyes as he looks down at the station from the bridge? Does the beggar die 'in lieu' of him? Does the giving away of the coat mark the giving away of fate? Is death physical annihilation, or just the loss of an identity marker? The sequence is rich in interpretative possibilities.

Another motif that was important to Guru Dutt's style was

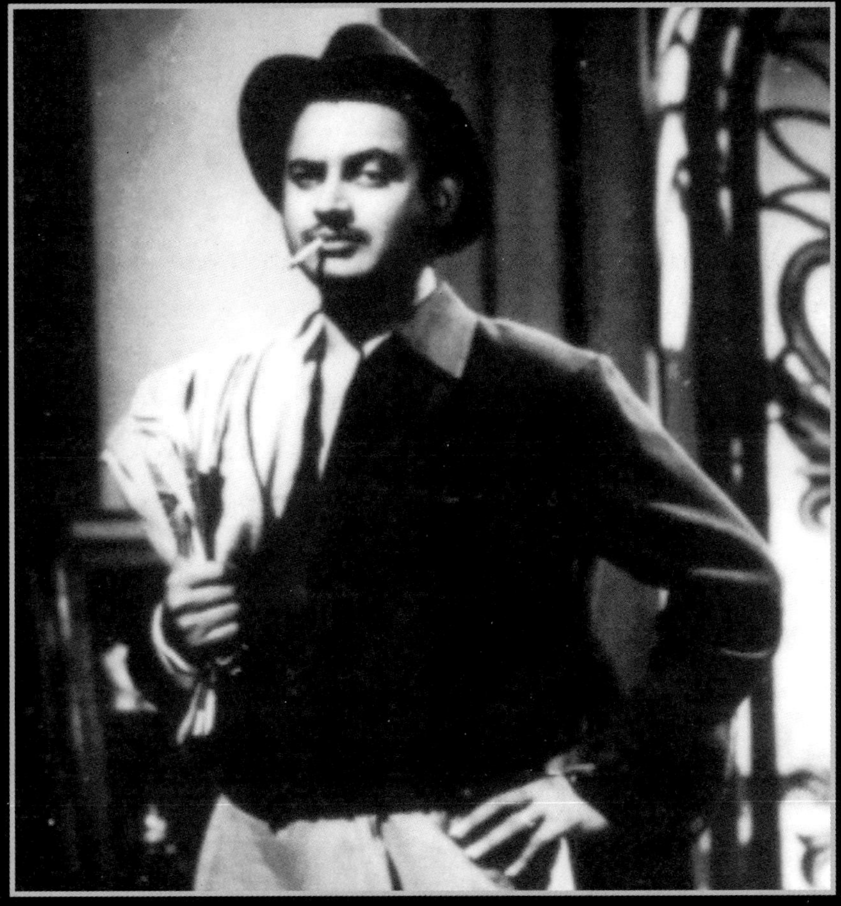

Guru Dutt in *Mr & Mrs 55*

the use of feet imagery. For Dutt, the feet were as important as any other part of the body, such as the face or the back. Characters or songs were often introduced through the feet. A shot, mid-sequence, could start from the feet. Shakila in *Aar Paar*, singing '*Babuji dheere chalna…*' is introduced through the feet; so is 'Captain', the don. Vijay's down-and-out status is evident in his worn out shoes in the bazaar street where he bumps into his mother. Bhootnath is introduced to Subinay Babu's household in *Sahib, Bibi aur Ghulam* through his squeaky new shoes. A contrast is set up between the feet of the nautch girl and wife: the dancer, Chote Babu is obsessed with, is introduced to us through her feet before she sings the song, '*Meri jaan, o meri jaan, achcha nahin itna sitam…*' And it is Choti Bahu's feet Bhootnath sees, before he sees her resplendent self.

One of the characteristic features of Dutt's style in song picturisation was the use of situational characters to express the feelings of the lead protagonists. The feelings have not been expressed to each other, or are as yet hazy and unacknowledged. In such a scene, Dutt uses situational characters who may not appear again in the film. Construction workers in *Aar Paar* sing *'Kabhi aar kabhi paar laga teer-e-nazar...'*; a passing toy-seller and her son sing *'Ab to ji hone laga...'* expressing an unexpressed bonding between the lead protagonists and later, a *qawaal* and his troupe sing *'Meri duniya lut rahi thi...'* in *Mr and Mrs 55* as Pritam leaves his wife's house after a showdown; *'Sun, sun, sun woh chali hawa...'* sing a chorus of revellers who follow Suresh Sinha and Shanti in their car in *Kaagaz ke Phool*; *'Aaj sajan mohe ang laga lo...'* sings a Baul singer in *Pyaasa*, expressing Gulab's longing for Vijay. It is this device of Dutt's that Raj Khosla also uses in two songs in *CID*: *'Bujh mera kya naam re...'* and *'Jadoo nagari se aaya hai koi jaadugar...'*, the first sung by village girls filling water from the river early in the morning, and the second by a street singer-couple. These songs tap, in Dutt's work, the repertoire of folk and other singing styles. There is, in the song sequence, a silent bonding of socially distinct groups: the protagonist, on the one hand, and the singers, on the other. Many of them point to a different social world where singing is part of and woven into the day's work. The only community song, where the lead protagonists participate in the fishing being done by the fisherfolk, is '*Jor lagake haiya…*' in *Jaal*.

Guru Dutt was also adept at picturising songs that were staged in workplace settings. '*Jaane kahan mera jigar gaya ji…*' in an office in *Mr and Mrs 55* where Johnny Walker romances a stenographer in the lunch break; Johnny Walker's '*Sar jo tera chakraye ya dil dooba jaaye…*' in *Pyaasa*; '*Sun sun sun zalima…*' in *Aar Paar* where Kalu Birju expresses his love for Niki in the garage that he works in; and '*Waqt ne kiya…*' in *Kaagaz ke Phool*, which unlike the other songs, is a song of separation, picturised in the studio where Shanti and Sinha work. In all these songs the place of work, or the work itself is an integral part of the song and its picturisation. Johnny Walker singing '*Yeh hai Bombay meri jaan…*' in *CID* is another leaf Raj Khosla

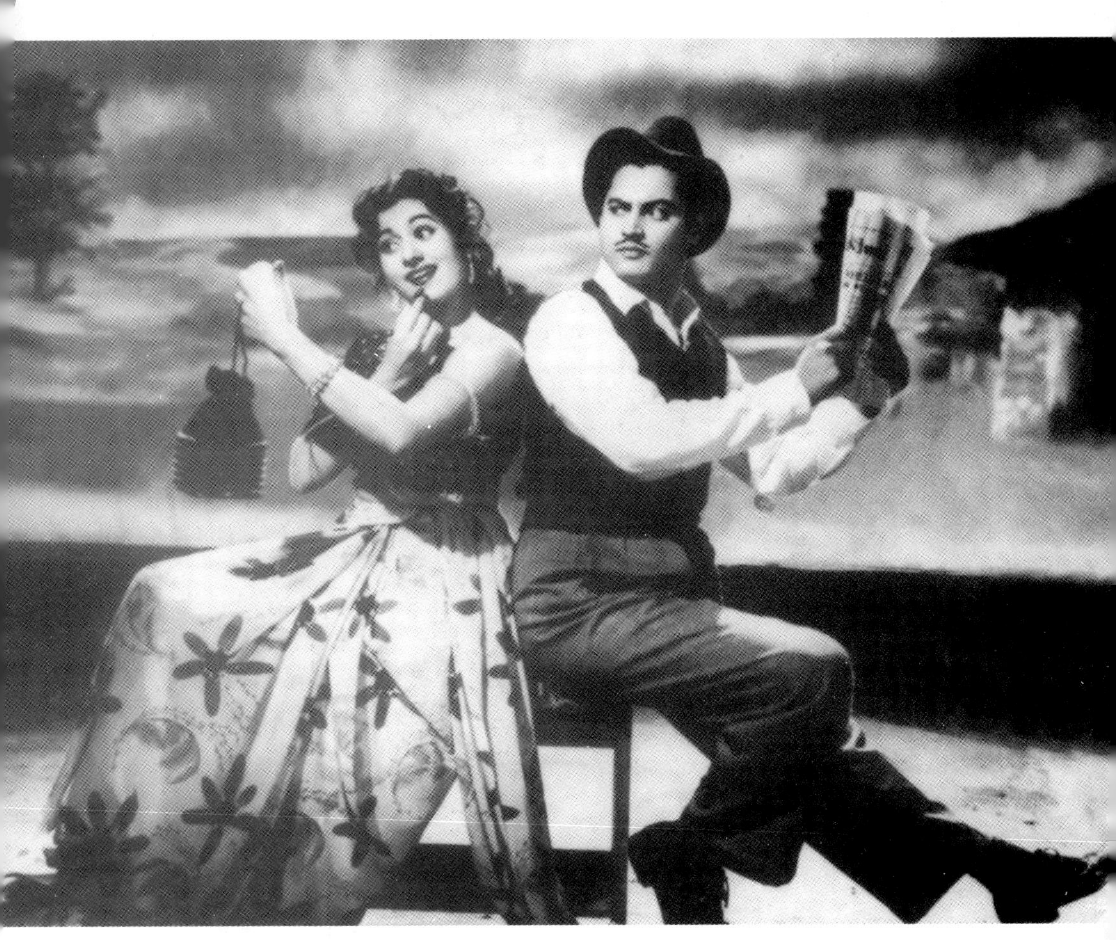

Madhubala with Guru Dutt in *Mr & Mrs 55*

took out of his mentor's style. The song is ironical, for it critiques the social mores of the city of Bombay and tells how difficult it is to live there, justifying the singer practicing his 'trade' of pickpocketing as he sings it!

Certain other motifs were repeated in the films. These include the umbrella songs in *Baazi* (Nina singing a song about rain in the night club) and Madhubala and her friends using umbrellas as sunshade in the song '*Thandi hawa, kali ghata...*' in *Mr and Mrs 55*. Dutt was also very fond of taxi and car drives with the lead protagonists across the city in *Baazi*, *Aar Paar* and *Kaagaz ke Phool*. The car as a framing device is used in a very innovative manner in '*Sun sun sun zalima...*' in *Aar Paar*. The song has been picturised with great fluidity in circular movements around the car and tracking movements with the windows of the car used as a framing device within these movements. (Guru Dutt's fascination for dancing is brought out in the walk that is a walk-and-dance step at the same time! The other song in his oeuvre where his talent for dance is showcased is the extended waltzing with Mala Sinha in the song *'Hum aap ki aankhon mein...'* in *Pyaasa*.) Raj Khosla uses this device of framing his characters through car windows in *'Pooch mera kya naam re...'* in *CID*.

Dutt's works also pose the question of whether authorship is just a name, as Foucault suggested, under which given texts are grouped, institutionalised and circulated. Here, too, there is a paradox —when Dutt renounced his name as the author, authorship functioned with redoubled energy, claiming him to be the 'author' of *Sahib, Bibi aur Ghulam*! Much in the manner of Vijay in *Pyaasa,* death and renunciation of identity as a director only rebounded to attach the texts even more emphatically to his name.

It is of importance that Guru Dutt never claimed the films to be his own. The act of 'gifting' had a sanctity that Guru Dutt did not violate in his lifetime. Whatever the reasons for asking M. Sadiq to make *Chaudhvin ka Chand,* it turned out to be the biggest commercial success among the films Dutt had produced. *Sahib, Bibi aur Ghulam* was a much awarded film and a film that was shown abroad. Despite this recognition, which none of his other films had received during his lifetime, Dutt, by all accounts, did not claim authorship of *Sahib, Bibi aur Ghulam*. The film can be referred to with the sign of an 'oblique' that would respect the implicated author of the work, as well as the gesture of 'gifting' that Dutt as producer and lead actor had undoubtedly made: Abrar Alvi/Guru Dutt.

Guru Dutt with Mala Sinha in *Pyaasa*

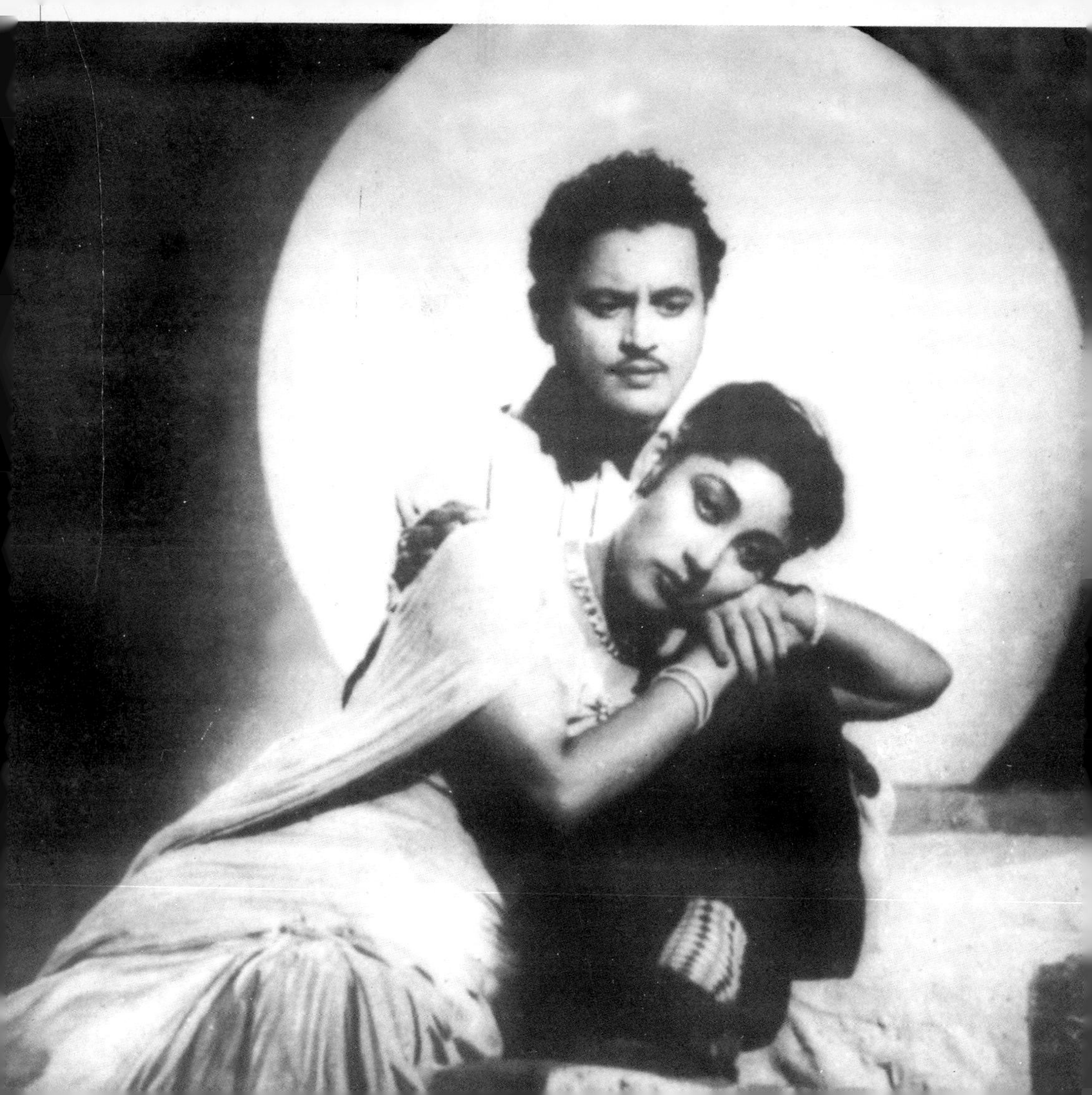

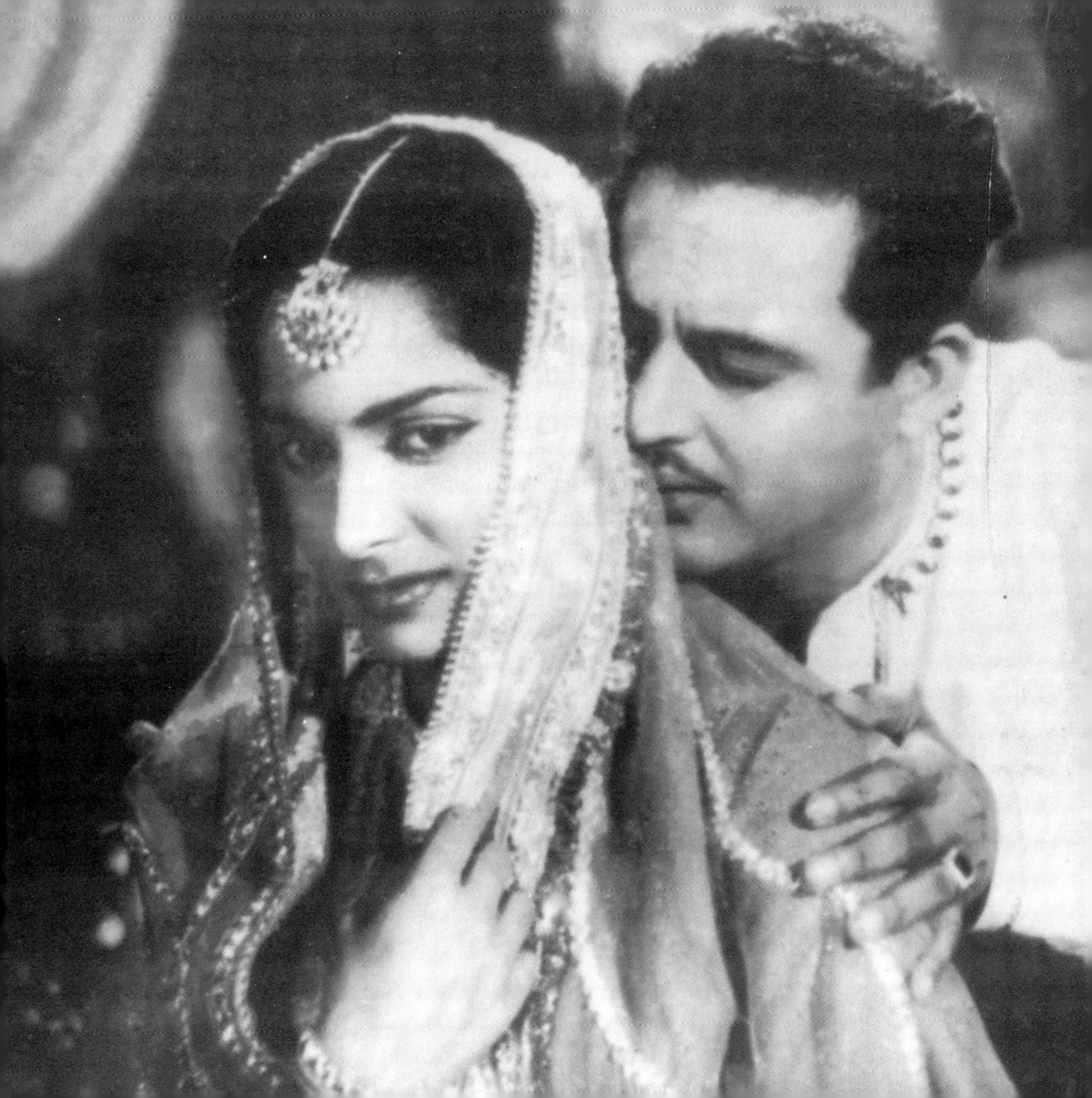

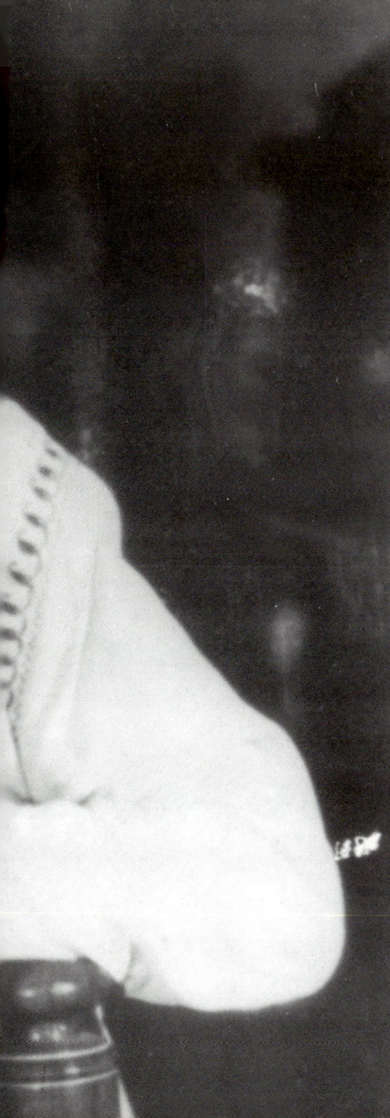

4

NARRATIVES OF HOMELESSNESS

Pyaasa, Kaagaz ke Phool and *Sahib, Bibi aur Ghulam* function as a kind of trilogy in much the same way that Ritwik Ghatak's trilogy on Partition – *Meghe Dhaka Tara* (1960), *Komal Gandhar* (1961) and *Subarnarekha* (1962) do. Unlike Satyajit Ray's Apu trilogy, which focused on Apu's passage into adulthood, Ghatak's trilogy dealt with the theme of the Partition of the sub-continent, without the plots of the three films being related to each other in any way. Dutt's three films, too, form a

Waheeda Rehman and Guru Dutt in *Chaudvin ka Chand*

set if considered from the point of view of the theme that runs through all of them— that of homelessness. If the films of the first phase had the lead protagonists establish a strong bonding with the street, from *Pyaasa* onwards the notion of home is problematised and assumes thematic-stylistic importance. If Vijay in *Pyaasa*, after he is thrown out of his brother's house, lives on the streets, *Kaagaz ke Phool* is about the dehoming of Suresh Sinha, the director, who lives in a huge house but has no home. Finally, he is out on the streets in utter poverty. Even Shanti, his actress, who is an orphan, sets up home in Bombay, only to renounce her career and home to keep a promise to Sinha's daughter. This 'dehoming' is a major theme of *Sahib, Bibi aur Ghulam* as well, in the tragic fate of Choti Bahu and in the demolition of the *haveli*, which marks the end of an era. It is of interest that *Pyaasa* refers to the post-Independence, post-colonial India; *Kaagaz ke Phool* is set in the period of transition (from the 1930s to the end of the 1940s); *Sahib, Bibi aur Ghulam* goes further back in time, and is set in the early 20th century. If Bhootnath is innocent and credulous, and in awe of the ways of the city and its people, Sinha tastes both adulation and rejection as filmmaker and moves from high self-esteem, bordering on arrogance, to despair, a complete loss of confidence and cynicism. (When Shanti arrives for the first time in Bombay, she is terrified by the camera mounted on a crane, coming her way in the studio; after Sinha's downfall, when he begins to lose his grip over filmmaking, he too cringes in a similar fashion, when he sees the camera approaching him.) *Pyaasa's* protagonist, in contrast to Suresh Sinha and Bhootnath, is already a hardened cynic, full of rebelliousness. *Kaagaz ke Phool* and *Sahib, Bibi aur Ghulam* share a similar structure: the narrative unfolds within the 'envelope' of a flashback of the lead protagonist, with a song that sets the mood and tone for the whole film. The three films also share engagement to melodrama in a very subtle and nuanced way.

Writing about Baudelaire's poetry, Walter Benjamin notes that the poet was taken up with the image of the flaneur, the stroller who walked the arcades of Paris, at home in the crowd. The flaneur was idle; his idleness was a challenge to bourgeois life which believed that industry, labour and production were the only legitimate markers of modern life. "In the flaneur the joy of watching is triumphant." If he were more observant while roaming, the flaneur would become a detective; if he were less so, he would be a mere gaper. The flaneur is more of a dandy. He is a product of modernity; he gives it legitimacy by watching it with a fine balance of detachment and intensity. "The street becomes a dwelling for the flaneur; he is as much at home among the facades of houses as a citizen is in his four walls. To him the shiny, enamelled signs of businesses are at least as good a wall ornament as an oil painting is to a bourgeois in his salon."

If the street was the home for the flaneur initially, it is the arcade later, that becomes a 'dwelling'. "If the arcade is the classical form of the *interieur*, which is how the flaneur sees the street, the department store is the form of the *interieur's* decay.

The bazaar is the last hangout of the flaneur. If in the beginning the street had become an *interieur* for him, now this *interieur* turned into a street, and he roamed through the labyrinth of merchandise as he had once roamed through the labyrinth of the city." The arcade is now the world within a world, where the flaneur experiences his own centrality while being anonymous in the fluid multitude that passes through it.

If the flaneur was the product of a European modernity, the colonial and post-colonial reality in India threw up its own kind of flaneurs. Since our modernity was 'different', our flaneurs, too, were different. *Pyaasa* and *Sahib, Bibi aur Ghulam* are two key works of the Hindi cinema that create our own contra-modern flaneurs. This is one more of the innovations that Guru Dutt's films gave to the Hindi cinema: the persona of the Indian flaneur. Vijay in *Pyaasa* has been forced to leave his brother's house; the street is his dwelling. It is from the street, its benches, parks and shopping lanes that he watches the life of the city, its wiles and guiles. It is here that he watches the streetwalker ply her trade; it is here that he meets an old college friend and her children; it is here that he carries the excessive and heavy shopping packages of the Sethji – a Sethji who seems to be somewhat sensitive when he wonders what times they are living through when educated people are forced to work as coolies – only to realise later that the coin he has given as payment is spurious. The intensity and detachment of the Baudelairian flaneur is present; so are the additional emotions of cynicism and the refusal to conform. If his poetry is that 'useless' labour that society can do without, he too refuses to house himself in its 'safe' dwellings. Watching is an integral part of the Bhootnath persona in *Sahib, Bibi aur Ghulam*. What both films offer is a view of that flawed modernity that colonialism and post-colonialism threw up, marking a traumatic transition from the feudal order to modernity. Bhootnath, like Vijay, does not have the arcade; but for him the huge *haveli* with all its wonders is no less than one. This is an *interieur* that the bumpkin from the village will never tire of watching and observing. The streets of the big city with its tall buildings gives him a crick in the neck. He strolls in the city and is witness to his brother-in-law's terrorist attack against the British; he also views with interest the Brahmo Samaji world of Jaba and her father. *Sahib, Bibi aur Ghulam,* in fact, offers a look at the paradoxical disjunctive segments of society and of a colonial modernity: Bhootnath, a simpleton from Fatehpur, is educated and more open to adapting to and learning the ways of the city than the feudal landlords in their sprawling mansions. Although located in the big city, they have no links with the changing world outside and its different set of values: they sign away, with a nonchalance born of ignorance, their property while engaged in a game of 'bird fight' with rival landlords.

Pyaasa is a sign-post in the history of Indian cinema for its conception of the street and in situating its homeless poet and streetwalker in its ambit. The Hindi film of the fifties, including the thriller, narrativises the split between home/sacred and non-home/profane spaces. *Pyaasa* is a truly radical film for the way it renders this split completely irrelevant. This is the only Hindi film that creates the street as a home for the protagonist through the duration of the entire narrative. The street was an important space in films of the post-Independence period, particularly in the films of the fifties starring Raj Kapoor and Dev Anand. The street is the place where the underdogs of the society live (*Kala Bazaar*); it is the space of love ('*Pyar hua, ikraar hua hai, pyar se phir kyon darta*

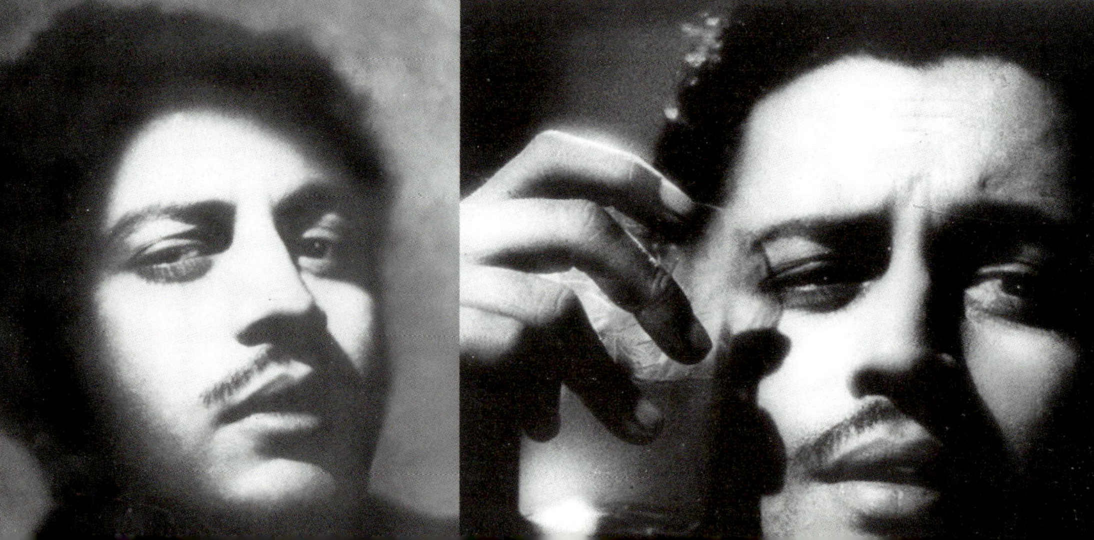

hai dil...' in *Shri 420*/1955); it is the space of irony (*'Rahne ko ghar nahin hai, sara jahan hamara...'* in *Phir Subah Hogi*/1958). But it is *Pyaasa* that makes the street the home, the space where the protagonist lives and goes into publishing houses, friends' homes, old college reunions, the *kotha*, a mental asylum, much as a wayfarer visits inns before he is on the road again. He is a flaneur, a stroller, who looks at life within the walls and from the street. It is on the street and not within homes that he gets his true recognition. The streetwalker or hair-oil masseur

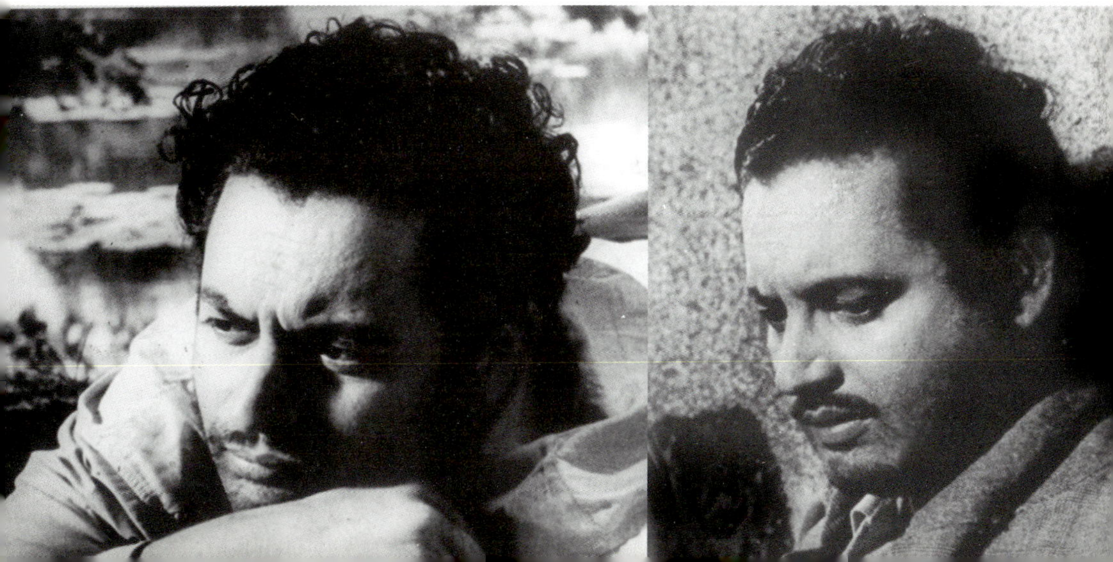

weaves her/his songs into her/his daily life, while those securely housed within four walls only see him as a business prospect.

The man on the street in our incomplete and disjunctive modernity is not the fashionable dandy of the European kind: the flaneur who enjoys looking at the city and its inhabitants as much as he enjoys being looked at. Of the actors of the fifties, the one who came closest to this Western conception of the flaneur was Dev Anand. He had a style, a free and-easy-going manner that bordered on dandyism. Raj Kapoor also belonged to the street but he cast himself more in the mould of the vagabond, drawing on the Chaplinesque tramp. The vagabond's character just is: he is not too deep into the business of looking. Guru Dutt creates a new kind of flaneur-spectator of and from the street. He is not a joyous type, but a cynical viewer. This is the kind of flaneur that 'our modernity' throws up. This is a protagonist from and on the street who is independent and passionate, but also aware of the power games people housed within walls play and the betrayals they are capable of. The protagonist of *Pyaasa* is 'everywhere at home' but he is a man against the crowd, not 'in the heart of the multitude'. This gesture of 'I against the crowd' is expressed directly with members of the crowd opposing him as in the reunion of old students in the college but is also treated cinematically by Dutt in the framing of the image with people turning back to look at the hero, Vijay. He is not within the frame of looks that bind the present and absent cinematic space in the frame. When he sings the prologue of the song '*Jaane woh kaise log the jinke pyar ko pyar mila...*', the people in the party turn over their shoulders to look at this curiosity of a servant who indulges in poetry. This creates a very uncomfortable feeling as the hero is not present in the frame when they look back and they are hence looking at the hero/the camera lens/the film audience! This over-the-shoulder look is maintained throughout the film: most of the sequences in the film begin with Vijay sitting on a bench at the harbour, in the park, on the street. Vijay sits with his back to the camera and it is only when he gets up that we see him. The very first sequence of the film establishes him as a spectator of the happenings of this world when we see him watching Nature and singing couplets. The over-the-shoulder look reaches its climax in the condolence meeting to mark his first death anniversary. Vijay enters through a back-lit entrance, Christ-like. In this sequence he brings his back-bench disruption tactics to fruition, reciting-singing his song '*Yeh mahalon, yeh takhton, yeh taajon ki duniya…*' even as the publisher, Mr Ghosh (actor Rehman) is conducting his sham proceedings from the stage. The audience in the huge hall starts looking back to see the singer. But this over-the-shoulder look and 'I against the crowd' theme comes to a climax in the sequence where Vijay is face-to-face with the crowd that has gathered to felicitate their beloved poet. Vijay, disgusted with the betrayal of his family and friends, announces that he is not Vijay. He renounces his identity just at the very point that fame is at his doorstep, thus pitting himself once again against the crowd, rather than going along with it. Guru Dutt makes his protagonist the ultimate spectator-flaneur: he watches his own death and effacement, not once, but twice-over.

This new conception of the hero in terms of the space he inhabits is not without significance vis-à-vis the women in the film. The heroine, Gulab (actress Waheeda Rehman), is a streetwalker. (It is important that she is not

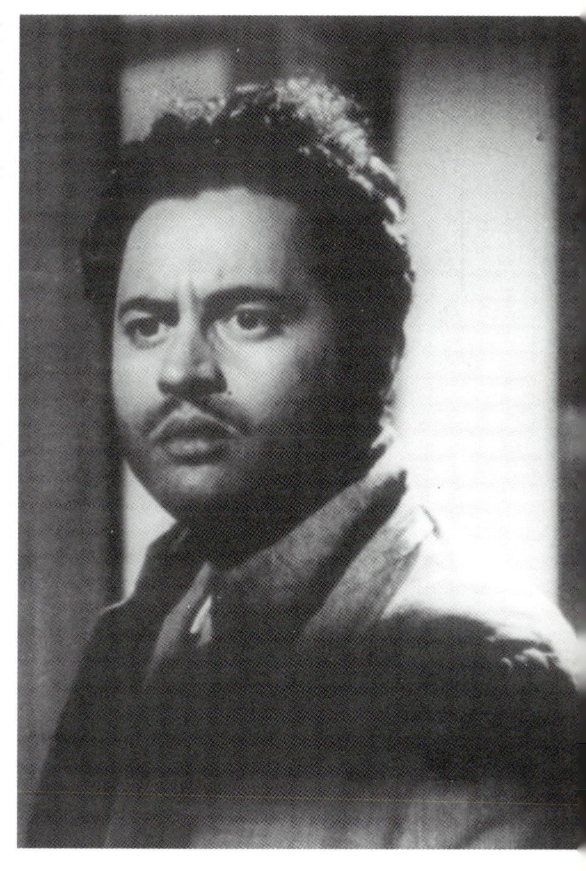

Guru Dutt in *Pyaasa*

'housed' in a *kotha*; she is not a gangster's mole either, 'housed' in a club or den. She is one of the few women characters in the Hindi cinema who actually walk the street.) She, too, is cast as a kind of a flaneur, a truly radical image in the Hindi cinema. "Woman cannot wander. The figure of the *flaneur* is traditionally male. A female equivalent was made difficult by a division of sexual realms that restricted female mobility and confined the woman into the space of the private." In the shot that establishes her, she stands up from the bench on the street, with her back to the camera, covered from head to toe by her sari. And yet, the way she stands and pulls up the strap of her bag on her shoulder and begins to sing a poem that is Vijay's, immediately establishes her character and profession. She meets him time and again on the street, and we see her walking the street, getting thrown out of a car, unpaid, being pimped for a rich businessman… She is as much of the street as the hero is, but she is more optimistic and despite her profession, not corrupted by cynicism. Even when she takes the poet into her room to recover from his drunkenness, there is no sense of enclosure. She sits at the open door while he sleeps on her bed. In a song sequence in which the song *'Aaj sajan mohe ang laga lo...'* sung by a group of street singers provides the ambience, Waheeda Rehman, completely overwhelmed by emotion goes after Guru Dutt, up the stairs of a house. The spectatorial desire to see the lead pair, who only meet on the street, finally 'housed' in privacy is once again belied, when we realise that the protagonist has actually ascended on to a terrace, again an open, unbounded space! *Pyaasa* is one of the rare films in the Hindi cinema where we are not given a 'history' of the heroine landing up on the streets. The narrative of her getting dehoused is never provided to us, with its accompanying rhetoric and melodrama. She just is; we need not know the why and wherefore.

To Guru Dutt goes the credit of picturising the most untitillating of *kotha* dances, in which the nautch-girl's movements are mechanically performed, torn as she is between earning her daily wages and looking after her sick and crying child. The claustrophobia of space, put-on emotion and the exploitative situation lead the protagonist to sing '*Jinhe naaz hai Hind par woh kahaan hai ...*' This is the ultimate contra-modern flaneur/spectator song, imbued with quiet despair, sorrow, disgust. The hero walks down the red light street, and we watch the 'little stories' unfold, as women are bought and sold, beckon, and still their persistent cough. 'Call the rulers of the land...' sings the hero, looking over his shoulders at the camera. Never has the fate of women and of the nation, and the angst of the artiste (poet on screen/director off screen) been so inextricably linked as in this powerful and radical sequence.

The song subverts all the generic images of the street that leads to the *kothas*. It is a sequence that puts the red-light area on display, as the hero takes a walk down it, singing about it. All the indexic markers of the red-light street that have been seen in many, many films are present here — the anonymous men who hurry in and out, the women who beckon provocatively... but in this song by Sahir Ludhianvi which is set to music by S.D. Burman, the tiredness and rotteness at the core of society is spectavised. Each stanza shows a different aspect of the red-light area: A woman comes up to Vijay; after seeing him, for some reason she walks away, covering her head with her saree (is it shame, or just the realisation that this drunken poet is no customer?); not so the girls who come up to him laughing and go away; the reference to the dancing bells and *tabla* (the sound-image of the *kotha,* encountered in countless

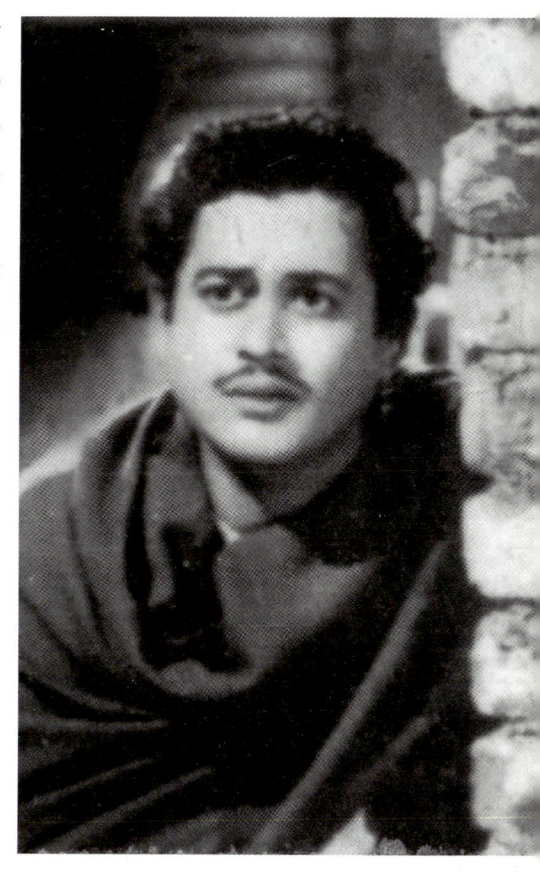

Guru Dutt in *Pyaasa*

films), is juxtaposed in image and sound with the reference to the sound of the cough…

Guru Dutt 'builds' up his themes in a systematic way, layering them with many significations. The song sequence '*Jinhe naaz hai Hind par woh kahaan hai…*' is preceded by three sequences which contribute to the song becoming one of the emotional high points of the film. Vijay, disturbed by the events of the previous day, is sitting at the harbour when he sees his estranged brothers perform some rituals. On asking, he finds out that his mother, who was very attached to him, is no more. The scene that follows is remarkable for being what Deleuze calls an optical-sound image— that is an image that goes beyond the cause-effect logic of classical narrative. Such images open up associations that are linked with subterranean stores of memory. Vijay remembers his mother asking him to take her along so that she could take care of him. He is on the threshold of a dark opening, a cluttered passage, which seems to have a staircase on the side. In front of this is water, the wet sand on the beach, and further down, the river. The foreground is dark and beyond is the shimmer of sand and water. This is the first of the two crucial scenes in which Vijay is at the threshold. (The second one is when he stands Christ-like, at the door of the auditorium where his first death anniversary is being observed.) Vijay is completely lost at the loss of his mother. The dark passage and glimmering water are ambivalent signifiers, evoking on the one hand, a sense of the womb and, on the other, of a threshold with death on the other side. Vijay then goes to a friend's house where he responds to his other friends' crude remarks by singing one of his poems. He then visits along with them a brothel, where the dancing girl is not allowed to attend to her sick and crying child. The loss of his mother and the plight of this other mother, leads him out to the red-light street where he sings '*Jinhe naaz hai Hind par woh kahaan hai...*' There is thus a gradual build up of the abstract image of 'motherhood' and 'womanhood', which is allegorised into the nation. The song metonymies the condition of the sick and persistently coughing women as a condition of the nation and state: in the final stanza of the song, Vijay, turning back over his shoulder, in characteristic fashion, asks that those who govern the state be called to answer for the sickness and rot of the society.

Pyaasa dares not only to debunk the notion of 'home', but to also not create any other space that offers security in lieu of home. The film never loses sight of the radical intent of its chronotope. It is in this context that the ending of the film should be seen. The hero and heroine walk hand in hand into the evening. It is a fictional space, and announces itself as such, even within the diegetic reality of the film. But the question that could well be asked is: Where else could the director have had them go, his hero having renounced his identity and refused the security of glory, fame and recognition? Where do the dehomed go, those who have turned their backs on the problematics of the home? They could have walked back on to the streets where they came from, but the hero has just pitted

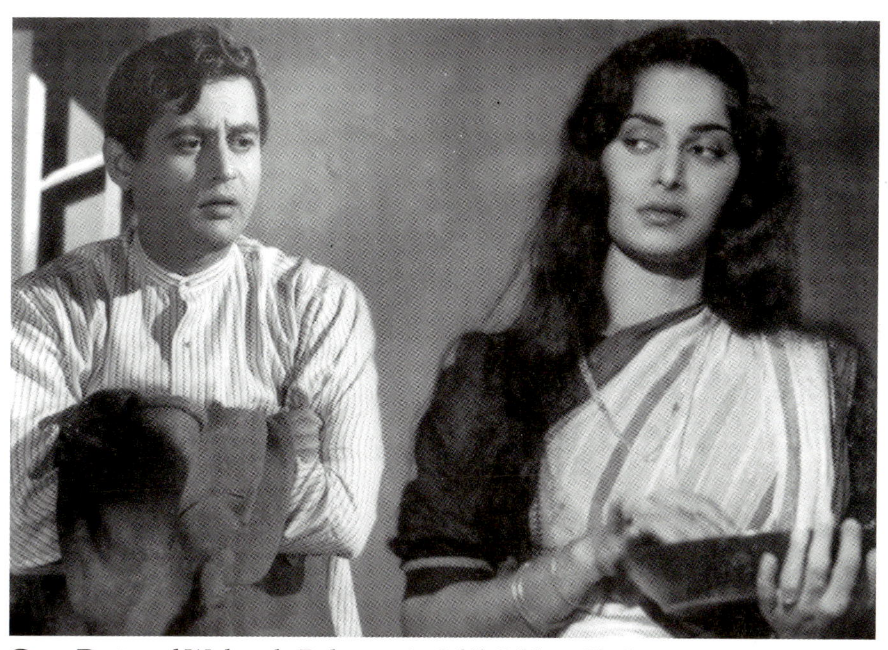

Guru Dutt and Waheeda Rehman in *Sahib, Bibi aur Ghulam*

himself once again against the crowd! The sunset, despite being a fictional and unreal entity, was probably the only space left that was neither a home nor a street.

Sahib, Bibi aur Ghulam by Abrar Alvi/Guru Dutt, has

another kind of an 'outsider' as its protagonist. Bhootnath has come from a small town, Fatehpur, to the big city of Calcutta. This is a period film set in the turn-of-the-century Bengal. (The remoteness of time, its passing and its literary origin is emphasised through the film by the images of Bimal Mitra's book being opened at the beginning and closed at the end of the film.) The crumbling of the feudal order, the modern enlightened ways of the Brahmo Samajis, and the terrorist ways of a section of the freedom movement – these are the facets of the social life that the wonderstruck, simpleton Bhootnath sees on his coming into the city. He is given a room to live in by his brother-in-law, who had taught in the big *haveli*. The room, whose window opens out on to the *haveli*, is visited by the servant of the house who is never too busy to come and give the latest news to this newcomer. So the point of view on the happenings in the narrative is that of the newcomer-outsider and the servant of the house. This joyous, gullible protagonist, soon endears himself to two very differently placed women: to Jaba (actress Waheeda Rehman), the daughter of the owner of Mohini Sindoor Factory where Bhootnath gets a job, and the youngest daughter-in-law (Choti Bahu, played by Meena Kumari) of the *haveli*. While Jaba, as the daughter of a liberated Brahmo Samaji, is fun-loving, teasing, and free in her social communication with others, Choti Bahu is completely hemmed in by the rules of the feudal house she lives in. She is as much an outsider to the ways of this house, as Bhootnath is, coming as she does from a poor family. Choti Bahu, unlike the other women of the house, wants her husband to stop going every night to visit dancing girls and stay with her. If Jaba expresses her desire playfully, singing '*Bhavra bada nadaan hai…*', Choti Bahu's desire is that of woman and wife. She, as she never fails to emphasise later, has performed the supreme sacrifice a wife can, for her husband. This articulation of her self-perception to her husband is in itself a radical gesture. Although her query about whether any other daughter-in-law of a Chaudhary household has done what she has done, may seem to be a rhetorical harping, it is in its own way a profound expression of her existential condition. What, then, is it this sacrifice that she keeps referring to? She allows her husband to force her to drink and tries to emulate the singing girls her husband visits every night. In this converting of the sanctity of her room into a *kotha*-like space, and the practice of seduction in the manner of the girls who sing and dance, the home itself becomes the space of profanation. The wife becomes an alcoholic, and the room in which the deity (God and husband) was worshipped now reeks of the pleasures of the flesh. The new-found indolence of Choti Bahu is well portrayed by the actress, director and cameraman, as the room seems to shrink into the space of the bed from which she seems unable to rouse herself. Bhootnath's first, and the spectator's first view of her, are of her bejewelled feet; terrified of her and this new situation he is in, he only sees her in 'parts'. The feet, the eyes, the seductive lips. But this deity-like sitting and standing form changes later to a lying or swaying form. When all her wiles and charm fail in enticing her husband up from the ground floor to her room even once during the day, she decides to become that which her husband sought elsewhere. Her husband, who is enamoured of her new self, actually devotes all his attention to her for several days. But his longing for the pleasures of the outside world finally overcomes him and he sets out. It is this effacement of her own being and beliefs to become other than her self that leads her to vocally protest at her condition. She sings a song, imploring him to stay '*Na jaao sainya…*' that is unique for its being almost entirely shot on the bed with the wife playing seductress. In the course of the song, she throws flowers at her husband, in a Janus-faced gesture of teasing and violence. When she realises that the husband will venture out no matter what, she protests. And it is this protest that is of interest. It borders on the trivial when she asks whether any other daughter-in-law has taken to drink to keep her husband home, but is resonant when she says, in reply to her husband's sarcastic query whether she is

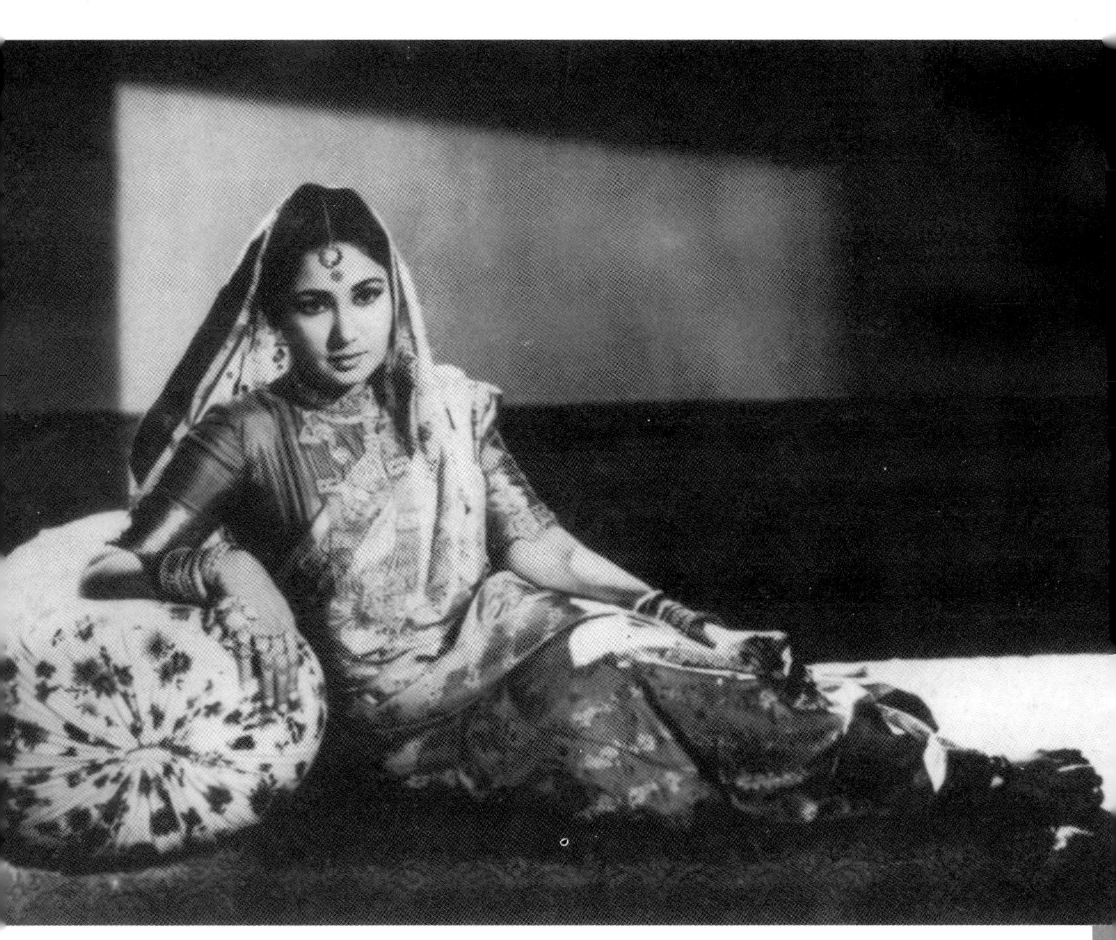

Meena Kumari in *Sahib Bibi aur Ghulam*

different because she has descended from the heavens: "Had I not been different, would I have suffered this sorrow?" This articulation of her difference from the other daughters-in-law of the house (who accept their husbands' 'hot blood' as a sign of belonging to a high caste) is almost philosophical, for in her persona the film carves an angst that cannot be contained or resolved by the situation she is in. Her final plea to her husband, having made profane that which was sacred, is equally tragic: "Take me to the *kotha*, change my name and keep me there," she says hysterically, before she collapses on to the floor. Few other films in the history of Indian cinema have caught this dilemma of the woman bound by home, and yet so alienated from it, so poignantly. Choti Bahu's intuitive perception of her situation, her articulation of her own desire, her questioning of her husband and his attitude towards her, internally ruptures the devoted wife-image that comes across very emphatically in her characterisation.

The point of view of the spectator, referred to earlier, that the protagonist exhibits, provides the organising principle for not just watching the facade of the city, or the mansion from the outside, but the interiors of the *haveli* as well. The narrative segment that is conceived as a journey within the *haveli* is unique in the complexity of its conceptualisation. After a trying encounter with Jaba, Bhootnath proceeds home. Choti Bahu has invited Bhootnath for the first time to her room. The narrative segment begins with the protagonist, full of trepidation, following the servant to Choti Bahu's room. On the way he secretly sees the eldest widow who keeps washing herself obsessively; he then meets Choti Bahu, which in itself opens a new world of femininity and suffering to him; on his way out he runs into Ghadi Babu, obssessed with clocks and the passing of time, and the only one of the brothers, who clearly sees that the feudal order has outlived its time. The last stop in this journey out of the *haveli* is at the door of the large room of the *haveli*, where the master of the house is having a troupe of dancing girls sing, '*Saqiyan aaj mujhe neend nahin aayegi…'* This journey through the house is also a journey through a whole new world for him that showcases the different faces of women: widow, cloistered daughter-in-law and the 'public' women. Guru Dutt in this sequence transforms the space of the house into an allegorical space for the different times of the nation. The decadent feudal order and its 'different times': the senseless immersion in ritual (the widow); Choti Bahu's 'non-conformist position', which does not accept the status quo; the mad brother, who in his madness is possessed of a wisdom; the lustful master of the house, wallowing in wine, women and song — all are part of the same sprawling mansion. A comparable sequence is to be found in Andrei Tarkovsky's *Mirror* (1974) in the sequence where the protagonist's estranged wife comes to leave their son with him for a few days. Each room opens up a 'different time of the Soviet Union': émigrés fleeing the Spanish civil war, an Akhmatova look-alike who makes the young boy read out the letter on the destiny of Russia by Pushkin to Chaadayev, the father's telephone conversation that takes father and son on a journey through the Second World War — the sequence ends with a powerful scene of the Soviet Union's face-off with China over the Damansky Island incident. While Tarkovsky opens up the house to a vast repertoire of memory-images of the nation, spanning decades and centuries, Abrar Alvi/Guru Dutt limit themselves to a realist conception of the unity of space and action. In both *Sahib, Bibi aur Ghulam* and *Mirror*, this allegorical construction of the nation through the space of the house stretches the concept of the 'sequence' to the limit: the separate 'times of the nation' are micro-sequences bracketed within a larger 'chapter' that makes a macro-sequence. This is a formal realisation of the theme of differing, even disjunctive, times existing within the nation.

The other interesting aspect of the structuring of the narrative is the way the mysterious ambience of the ghost film is woven into this story about the crumbling feudal social formation. The film begins with a greying Bhootnath supervising the demolition of a *haveli*. As he begins to hear the first few words of the song, '*Chale aao…*' with a ghostly echo, we realise he shares deep bonds with this place. This haunting call is reinforced as the flashback begins, when he hears the song in the still of the night. The voice, which is unattached to a body, flows through the *haveli*. The address is paradoxical for it refers to itself in third person: '*Koi door se awaaz de chale aao…*'. The *koi* (someone), as we learn later, is Choti Bahu herself, singing of her lonely nights and her own desire. Or is *she* being called by a stranger? This ghostly ambience is reinforced by Hemant Kumar, who has scored unforgettable, haunting tunes for this film, and was himself a film and music director fascinated by the mystery genre. This call, unaddressed to any specific person, interpellates the newcomer, who is bound by it. Choti Bahu's relationship with him is near-motherly, but also slightly seductive and blackmailing. It is she who hides him in a secret cellar in the women's section of the mansion, a 'womb' of the house, as she nurses him in a motherly way back to health, when he breaks his leg. "You care for me very much, don't you? Then, get me alcohol," she orders him later. "You are the only person who understands me," she tells him in the carriage on her first and last journey from her confining home. His 'understanding' is actually his spectatorial status, that allows him as an affectionate outsider to view the passing of an age and the 'small' but piercing tragedy of a woman who rebels in loneliness, trying to efface the distinctions of the mutually exclusive spaces of the sacred and the profane, of displeasure within the home and pleasure without that her husband obsessively sought, night after night. Though firmly grounded in her room in the sprawling mansion, and later bound to the bed in the room as an alcoholic, she is a homeless soul. This only makes more poignant the finding of her skeleton, in that very secret cellar of the mansion that Bhootnath, years later, is having pulled down.

Guru Dutt and Meena Kumari in *Sahib, Bibi aur Ghulam*

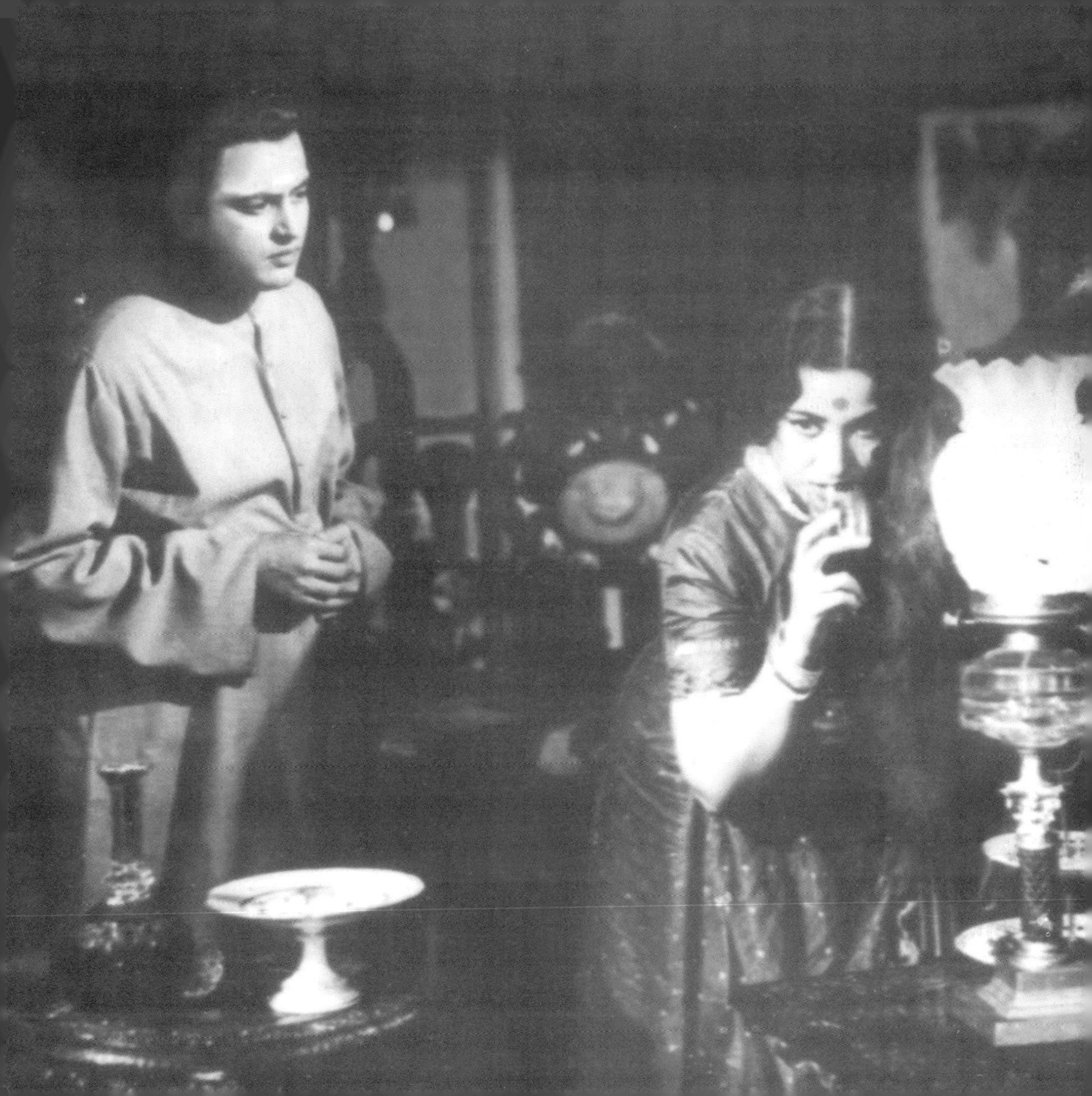

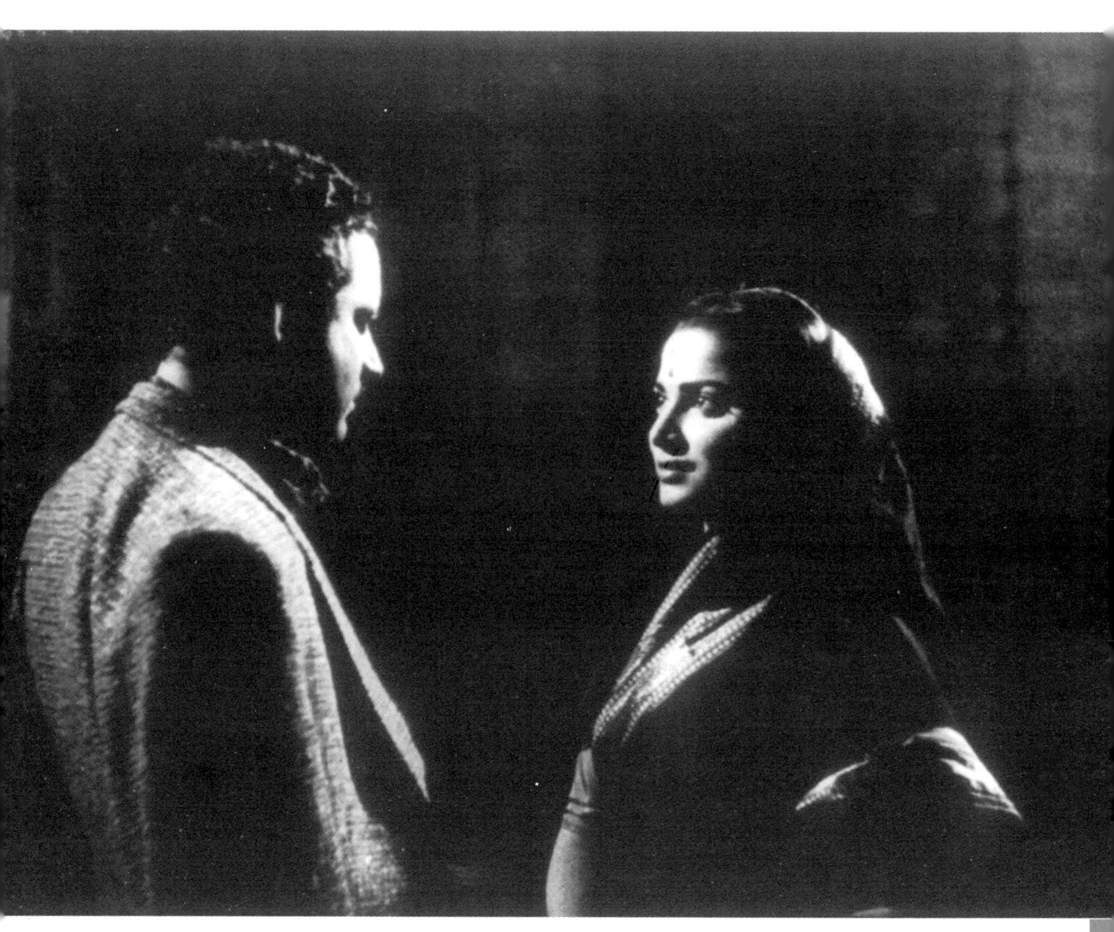

Guru Dutt and Waheeda Rehman in *Kaagaz ke Phool*

5

PASSING THROUGH LIGHT, PASSING THROUGH SHADOWS

Guru Dutt was a director who took the words 'black-and-white film' very literally, and very philosophically. The image for him was a play of darkness and light and he, along with his cinematographer, V.K. Murthy, experimented with the many ways in which this play could take place. In fact, he is one director – and probably the only one in the Hindi cinema – who actually, every once in a while, shades the part of the face that is considered 'the window to the soul'. Guru Dutt does this through the use of shadow, as in the scene when the old Sinha Sahib is descending the stairs after having gone over his studio in *Kaagaz ke Phool*, where the moving black shadow that covers his face portends his death; or by having the protagonist actually cover the eyes at a crucial moment with her hands as the dancer in the red-light area in *Pyaasa* does. Mala Sinha, lying on the divan in *Pyaasa*, covers her eyes with her hand in an important emotional confrontation with Guru Dutt. The contrast of light and shade on the face is normally used to 'cut' the face vertically into two halves in dramatic moments of the narrative; Dutt uses light and shade horizontally to shade the top part of the face including the eyes, while the lower part is lit.

In the works of Dutt-Murthy-Chawhan (for the fluidity of movement that Dutt's work is known for is as much due to the camera as due to the editing), there is a coming together of a very deep and profound grounding in Indian melodrama and the performative modes of the Hindi cinema along with a fascination for Hollywood, particularly the grandeur and scale of an Orson Welles, and a predilection for realism from the British cinema (and probably from the European cinema as well).

In Dutt's melodrama, as in Ghatak's, it is the melodic

structuring of narrative that predominates, rather than drama. The dramatic tensions are always understated in the enactment by the actors; there is often an intelligent use of 'distantiation' through mise en scene. Space is opened up through a variety of devices when emotion threatens to spill over. The effect is not one of 'containing' this flowing emotion, but of spreading it across a larger canvas to give it a deeper melancholic and mellow feel. Two important sequences in this respect are the '*Aaj sajan mohe ang laga lo…*' song in *Pyaasa* and '*Waqt ne kiya…*' in *Kaagaz ke Phool*. In the first song, we follow Gulab, as she, overwhelmed by Vijay's noble gesture of saving her from the police, follows Vijay up a staircase. Vijay is a little ahead; he obviously intends to sleep on the terrace for he is carrying his bedding. He has had a trying day and is so completely lost in thought that he is unaware of her presence. The percussion in the song reaches a crescendo, and there is a quick rhythm in the cutting, with the camera receding from the two protagonists being shown separately. Suddenly, there is an opening out of space on the terrace with the figures shown together in the same frame. This shot subtly changes the mood from trepidation and urgency to hesitation and restraint on Gulab's part. (This is followed by the segment in which she goes close to him, nearly lays her head on his back and then leaves him silently.)

'Waqt ne kiya kya haseen sitam...' in *Kaagaz ke Phool* also begins with the director walking into the studio in a beam of light. He talks to Shanti (actress Waheeda Rehman) who has arrived in the studio even before him. When he asks her who she is knitting the sweater for, she replies playfully in a low-angle mid-shot, a little to the side, that it is for someone as lonely as she is. In a great cut to the back of the protagonists, we see Suresh Sinha/Guru Dutt walking away from the camera into the depth of the frame. This sudden distancing, change of angle and opening up of the space of the frame on to the studio, is the prologue to the moving song that in one of those ironies of cinema encapsulates the emotional triangle of wife-man-beloved in diegetic and non-diegetic space. The song begins as

Guru Dutt and Waheeda Rehman in *Kaagaz ke Phool*

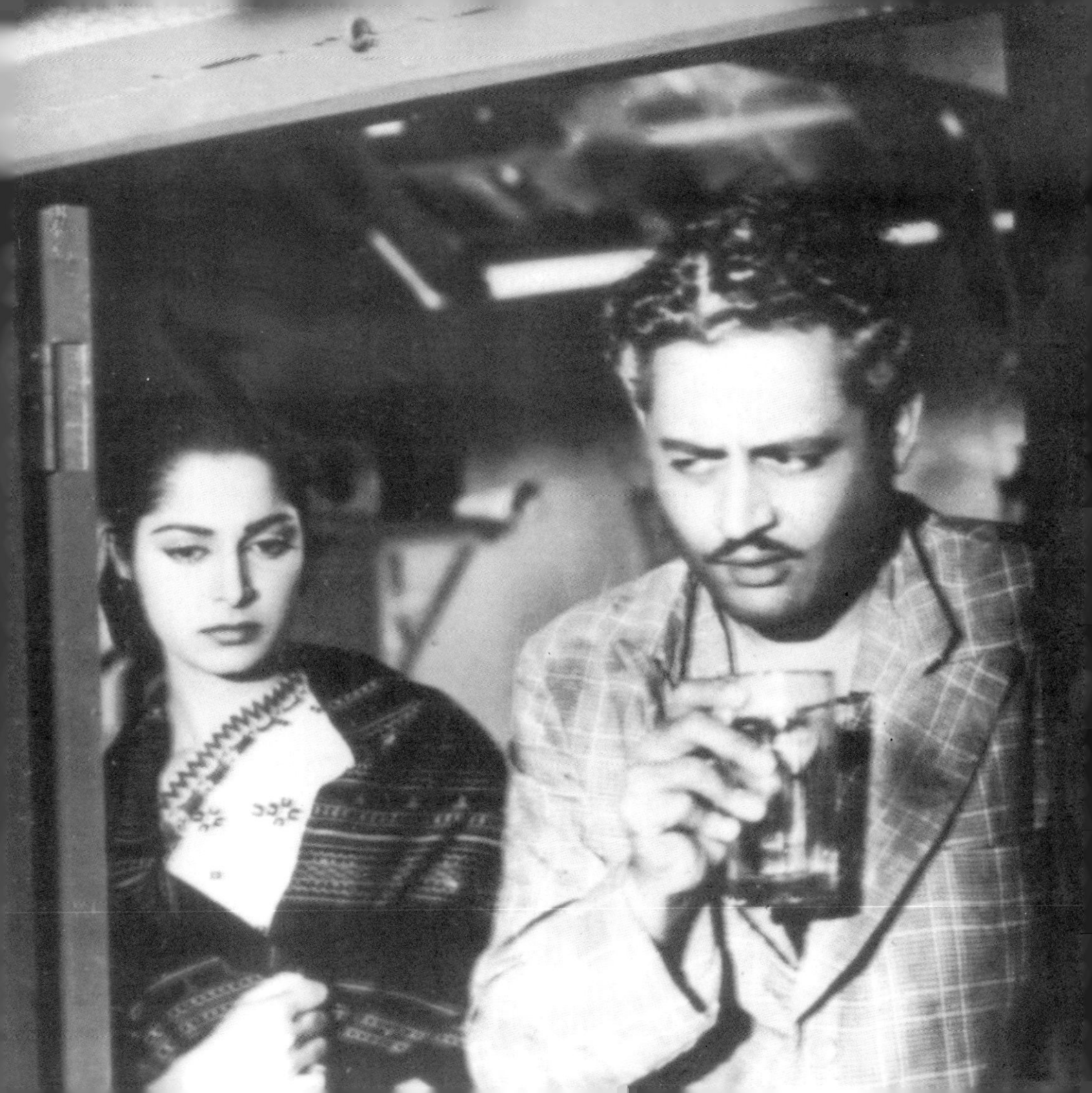

Dutt tells her that he is a married man. The playback singing for the song was done by Dutt's wife in real life, Geeta Dutt. This is probably one of the most poignant moments of autobiographical revelation by a director in love with his heroine in any cinema anywhere ever. The revelation as an embedding in the folds of the narrative, increases the tragic intensity of the sequence manifold. Waheeda Rehman's face moves through the slabs of light and darkness and both of them are caught in a beam of light that only emphasises the divergence of two destinies during the song. Dutt also creates an unusual effect where at a moment in the song, Waheeda Rehman's face is so harshly lit that even the upper contours of her cheeks under her eyes are visible. Her face looks more like a mask in this shot. This kind of lighting makes the imagic aspect of the face all the more apparent. Waheeda Rehman stands in a stylised pose that is not cinematic but photographic or painterly in essence (the rich black of the saree she is wearing only highlights this effect), before she hugs to her bosom the knitting and knitting needles. The studio where the song is picturised, the spotlights and props are used very evocatively.

The melodic component is used by Dutt in *Pyaasa*, *Kaagaz ke Phool* and *Sahib, Bibi aur Ghulam* to structure the narrative. Songs here hold the sequences together and loop in previous narrative segments. '*Koi door se...*' in *Sahib, Bibi aur Ghulam* is an example of such a melodic structuration. In *Kaagaz ke Phool*, the film begins after the titles with the old Sinha Sahib entering the studio, in a beam of light. While the entire story of many films (such as Mehboob's *Mother India* and Yash Chopra's *Deewar*) unfolds through the flashback, this is one film where the flashback sequence occurs through the song '*Dekhi zamane ki yaari...*' within the envelope of which the whole film unfolds. The flashback to a time when this old man was a young, successful director, begins with the stanza '*Waqt hai meherbaan...*' In the last narrative segment of the flashback, Sinha, working as a mere extra, is unable to deliver his lines because he sees that the heroine, dressed as a *jogan*, is none other than his beloved Shanti. He runs out on to the street, with an elemental wind blowing, chased by Shanti who recognises him. The song, *'Ud ja, ud ja, pyaase bhavre…'* begins, which turns out to be a stanza of the song we heard in the beginning, *'Dekhi zamane ki yaari…'* as we return to the old Sinha Sahib in the studio.

Apart from the taste for melodrama, Dutt shared another similarity of sorts with Ritwik Ghatak. The use of a panoramic scale, depth of focus, and framing are rarely balanced in the Western sense. There is usually a tilt in the angle, high or low, though not as pronounced as it was in Ghatak's. There is also the fascination, as with Ghatak, with playing with differential planes in the frame. One of the early examples of multiple planarities is in the opening sequence of the song *'Babuji dheere chalna…'* in *Aar Paar*. In Guru Dutt's films scale is used very dramatically as in the opening sequences of *Kaagaz ke Phool* and *Sahib, Bibi aur Ghulam*. Scale and planarity are used to effect to show the final break between Vijay and Mina in *Pyaasa*. Vijay gets up from a bench to drink water from a tap. He looks up and from this bent posture sees in the distance, Mina (actress Mala Sinha) climb out of a huge car to possibly talk to him. A train passes by between them, cutting them spatially from each other.

Murthy's camera moves along with Dutt's cinema. In the early work, there is the fascination for movement, for texture and light and shade. Throughout his work with Dutt, Murthy experimented with circular and planar movements and with tracking and deep focus. However, it is with the trilogy, that a grand thematic conception dovetails with the grandeur of the image created by a complex orchestration of the movement of light and shade. In the trilogy, Murthy's tracks have evolved to incorporate the sense of looking, of 'spectating' (for characters such as Vijay and Bhootnath). The tracks also convey a sense of the passage of time as necessitated by the fictional biographies Dutt was taking up. The tracks and lighting also show a sensitivity to the tragic destinies of the protagonists. In

Choti Bahu's room, for instance, in *Sahib, Bibi aur Ghulam*, even the darkness is luminous.

The aesthetics of the Dutt-Murthy combine seem to reflect a belief that light and shade were the *yin* and *yang* of life. A passing through light, only meant there would now be a passing through shade. The opposite was equally true. If there was a passage through darkness, there would thereafter be light. The passage through light and shade with the knowledge that both were part of a larger flux, is the underlying principle of their work. Expressionism encapsulated the conflict between good and evil through light and darkness that seemed to impart a cruel life even to inorganic objects such as walls, doors, streets. In noir films, light and shade added to the sense of mystery, suspense and gloom. In Dutt's films, particularly in the later works, light and darkness assume a distinct presence all their own with characters and their destinies passing through them.

If black and white was explored by Guru Dutt as light and shade, it was also explored as shafts and beams of light, and patches of darkness. Dutt's preoccupation with light and darkness never became expressionistic precisely because the patches and patterns he created lacked weight and opacity. They were neither sharply contrastive, nor static or angular. They were usually always in movement. Since Dutt-Murthy's work is infused with the belief that light and shade are two sides of the same mode of being, light always moves gently into darkness and vice versa.

It was in the song sequences that this preoccupation reached fruition as light and darkness in emotive movement. '*Meri baat rahi mere man mein…*' in *Sahib, Bibi aur Ghulam* has the heroine's face going into darkness as she recollects happy moments with Bhootnath in the past. In the song, '*Jaane kya tu ne kahi…*' in *Pyaasa*, Waheeda Rehman's face, as she moves from under architectural structures to the other side, the shadow of the arch falls over and moves across the face. The play of light and shade continues all through the song, on benches and colonnades, through back streets and alleys. All through the song she looks back, beckoning Guru Dutt.

The song *'Saakiyan aaj mujhe neend nahin aayegi...'* in *Sahib, Bibi Ghulam* is unique for its picturisation in keeping only the main dancer in light and the accompanying dancers constantly in shadow, even when the dancers are in movement all across the wide floor or even in medium close-up. The 'extra' dancers are in a shadow slab while the musicians behind them and the dancer in front of them are in light. This song takes the notion of movement of object – in this case, the dancers – and the movement of the camera to new heights, because there is the three-tiered lighting system at work too! In addition, there is moving light and shade being cast by the huge cloth 'fan' hung from ceiling in gently swaying up and down movements. (This 'cloth fan' has also been used in the *'Meri jaan, o meri jaan...'* song in the same film.) Such a grand orchestration of camera, light and actors in movement has rarely been seen in the Hindi cinema.

Dutt and Murthy used the beam of light very innovatively. In their use, this light is not revelatory; it is a use that has been made in a variety of genres including science-fiction, where the alien usually enters in a strong beam. The beam is now used in the commercial Hindi film to herald the entry of the avenging hero or the villain on a devastation spree, or an interrogation set-up in the police station. Dutt's use is unique, for it serves neither as a revelation nor as a focusing device vis-à-vis the narrative. His beam of light is benign; it bathes the protagonist in grace. Characteristically, in *Kaagaz ke Phool*, Sinha Sahib dies sitting in the director's chair, next to a beam of light, with a few rays falling over him, and as the door opens to let the studio workers in, we are again witness to a large patch of moving light as it enters the studio. The beam is not *on* him in a rhetoric gesture, but almost stands guard by his dead body, graciously.

Guru Dutt passed from light to darkness at a young age. The works he left behind, however, even half a century after they were made, continue to enthrall viewers with the very personal vision of their maker.

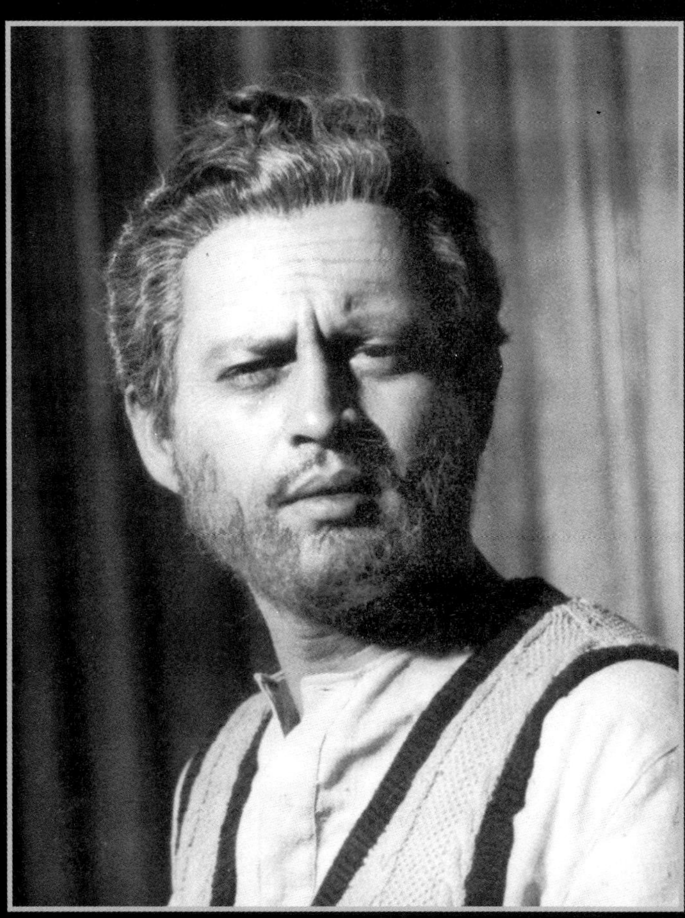

Guru Dutt in *Kaagaz ke Phool*

SONGS

'Aaj sajan mohe ang laga lo': Today, beloved, hold me close…

'Ab to ji hone laga kisi ki surat ka saamna': Now that one has to face someone's face…

'Babuji dheere chalna, pyaar mein zara sambhalna': Tread carefully, man, keep a hold on yourself in love…

'Dekhi zamane ki yaari, bichde sabhi bari bari': I've seen the friendliness of this world, everyone has left, one by one…

'Hum aap ke aankhon mein is dil ko basa le to': What if my heart were to settle down in your eyes…

'Jaane kahan mera jigar gaya ji': I wonder where my heart has gone off to…

'Jaane kya tu ne kahi, jaane kya maine suni, baat kuch ban hi gayi': Whatever it was that you said, whatever it was that I said, something anyway could be made of it…

'Jaane woh kaise log the jinke pyar ko pyar mila': What kind of people were they, who managed to get love in return for love…

'Jinhe naaz hai Hind par woh kahaan hai': Where are they who take pride in India…

'Jor lagake haiya, paon dabake haiya': Use your strength, dig your feet in…

'Kabhi aar kabhi paar laga teer-e-nazar': The arrows of the glances of love hit this way at times, and at other times, that way…

'Koi door se awaaz de chale aao': Someone calls from the distance, come to me…

'Jadoo nagari se aaya hai koi jaadugar': A magician has come from the land of love…

'Meri baat rahi mere man mein': My thoughts remained unspoken…

'Meri duniya lut rahi thi aur main khamosh tha': My world was being looted and I was silent…

'Meri jaan, o meri jaan, achcha nahin itna sitam': Beloved, o my beloved, such cruelty is not good…

'Na jaao saiya': Don't leave me, beloved…

'Bujh mera kya naam re': Guess what my name is…

'Pyar hua, ikraar hua hai, pyar se phir kyon darta hai dil': We have fallen in love and expressed it, so why then is the heart scared of love…

'Rahne ko ghar nahin hai, sara jahan hamara': We have no house to dwell in, yet the whole world is ours…

'Saqiyan aaj mujhe neend nahin aayegi': O winebearer, I shall not be able to sleep today…

'Sar jo tera chakraye ya dil dooba jaaye': When you are giddy or feeling down…

'Sun sun sun zalima': Listen, listen, listen to me, you cruel one…

'Sun, sun, sun woh chali hawa': Listen to the wind blowing…

'Thandi hawa, kali ghata': Cool breeze, black clouds…

'Ud ja, ud ja, pyaase bhavre': Fly away, fly away, thirsty bee…

'Waqt hai meherbaan': Time is indulgent…

'Waqt ne kiya kya haseen sitam, tum rahe na tum, hum rahe na hum': Time dealt us such exquisite blows, you could not remain yourself, neither could I…

'Yeh hai Bombay meri jaan': This is Bombay, my dear…

'Yeh mahalon, yeh takhton, yeh taajon ki duniya': This world of palaces, thrones and crowns…

FILMOGRAPHY

As Assistant Director

1945

Lakhrani (directed by Vikram Bedekar)

1946

Hum Ek Hain (We are One, directed by P. L. Santoshi)

1947

Mohan (directed by Anandinath Banerjee)

1949

Girl's School (directed by Amiya Chakravarty)

1950

Sangram (The Struggle, directed by Gyan Mukherjee)

As Director

1951

Baazi (The Gamble, aka The Wager)

1952

Jaal (The Net)

1956

Sailaab (The Flood)

As Director, Producer, Actor

1953: *Baaz* (The Hawk / H. G. Films)

1954

Aar Paar (This Side or the Other, aka Heads or Tails, Cupid's Arrow / Guru Dutt Productions)

1955

Mr & Mrs 55 (Guru Dutt Films Ltd)

1957

Pyaasa (The Thirsting One, aka The Seeker, Eternal Thirst / Guru Dutt Films Pvt Ltd)

1959

Kaagaz ke Phool (Paper Flowers / Guru Dutt Films Pvt Ltd)

As Producer

1956

CID (directed by Raj Khosla)

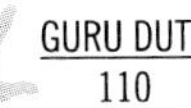

As Producer, Actor

1960

Chaudvin ka Chand (Fourteenth Day of the Moon, aka Full Moon, directed by M. Sadiq)

1962

Sahib, Bibi aur Ghulam (Master, Mistress and Slave, aka King, Queen and Knave, directed by Abrar Alvi)

As Actor

1958

12 o' clock (directed by Pramod Chakravorty)

1962

Sautela Bhai (Step-brother, directed by Mahesh Kaul)

1963

Bahurani (Daughter-in-law, directed by T. Prakash Rao)

1963

Bharosa (Trust, directed by K. Shankar)

1964

Sanjh aur Savera (Dusk and Dawn, aka Evening and Morning, directed by Hrishikesh Mukherjee)

Suhagan (Married Woman, K.S. Gopalakrishnan)

Unfinished Films as Actor

Baharen Phir Bhi Aayengi (Spring Will Arrive, Nonetheless; replaced by Dharmendra)

Love and God (replaced by Sanjeev Kumar)

Unfinished Productions

Professor

Raaz (The Secret)

Gouri

Kaneez (The Slave-girl)

NOTES AND REFERENCES

Publisher's Note: The author's original manuscript had superscripts within the text. To make the book friendlier to non-academic readers, we have decided to publish the notes in the following format —

Page 1 (lines 6-9): Atmaram quoted in *Guru Dutt: A Life in Cinema*, Nasreen Munni Kabir, OUP, Delhi, 1996, p. 7. Henceforth this book is referred to as GDLC.

Page 2 (lines 3-7): Ibid.

Page 5 (reference to 'troubled love-life' in line 8): Dutt's fascination for the leading lady of many of his films, Waheeda Rehman, is well known.

Page 5 (reference to 'suicide' in line 11): Lalitha Lajmi, Dutt's sister, speculates whether it was death due to natural causes or suicide: "Guru Dutt was lying in a peculiar position when he died.

His leg was lifted, it was as though he was about to get up from the bed. There was an unfinished Hindi novel by his bedside, the lights were on. It was like a frozen moment. … It's a big question whether it was suicide or whether it had been heart failure in his sleep. One still doesn't know, but probably it was intentional." GDLC, p. 129.

Page 7 (last line) - page 8 (lines 1-13): 'The Great Four of the Golden Fifties', Iqbal Masud, in *Frames of Mind: Reflections on Indian Cinema*, Aruna Vasudev (ed.), Special Issue of Indian Horizons, Vol. 44, No. 1, ICCR, New Delhi, 1995, pp. 29-30.

Page 12 (lines 7-9): GDLC, p. 37.

Page 23 (lines 15-18) - page 24 (lines 1-7): 'The Great Four of the Golden Fifties', Iqbal Masud, in *Frames of Mind: Reflections on Indian Cinema,* Aruna Vasudev (ed.), Special Issue of Indian Horizons, Vol. 44, No. 1, ICCR, New Delhi, 1995, p. 36.

Page 25 (lines 9-14): GDLC, p. 66.

Page 26 (lines 14-18) - page 27 (lines 1-5): GDLC, p. 130.

Page 30 (reference to 'personal stamp' in line 6): "Jean-Louis Commolli: … American cinema, basically, is not an auteur cinema: the reverse of European cinema. Auteurs in American cinema are exceptions; the rule they confirm is not that of a consistency and invariability in their work, but of their extreme fragility, complexity and formal plasticity." 'Twenty Years On: 1965', Jean-Louis Commolli et al, in *Cahiers du Cinema: 1960-1968*, Jim Hillier (ed.), Harvard University Press, Massachusetts, 1986, p. 204.

Page 30 (lines 13-18) - page 31(lines 1-7): 'Sunspots', Fereydoun Hoveyda in *Cahiers du Cinema: 1960-1968*, Jim Hillier (ed.), Harvard University Press, Massachusetts, 1986, p. 142.

Page 31 (lines 15-17): 'On the politique des auteurs', Andre Bazin in *Cahiers du Cinema*, Jim Hillier (ed.),Vol. 1, Routledge and Kegan Paul, London, 1985, p. 255.

Page 34 (lines 3-11): 'Ghatak and Guru Dutt', Arun Khopkar, *Cinemaya 13*, Autumn 1991, p. 60.

Page 37 (reference to *Sahib, Bibi aur Ghulam* in line 15): Writers on cinema, when writing on Guru Dutt, take it for granted that *Sahib, Bibi aur Ghulam* belongs to Guru Dutt. For instance, "In none of Guru Dutt's other tragic melodramatic works does the conflict between historic circumstance and personal compulsions emerge as powerfully as it does in this film (i.e. *Sahib Bibi aur Ghulam* - RD)." 'In the Realm of Shadows', Arun Khopkar, *Journal of Arts and Ideas*, January-March 1983.

Page 37 (reference to *Chaudhvin ka Chand* in line 16): For instance, "Emotionally rich, laden with haunting melodies films like *Eternal Thirst* ... and *Fourteenth Night of the Waxing Moon* fired the imagination of the public and have stood the test of time as well. He brought the Bengali ethos with him but stood apart from this or any other trend of the times. He was a loner, a poet, a filmmaker with an instinctive feeling as much for mood and atmosphere as for the rhythm and flow of images.... In films like *Eternal Thirst, Paper Flowers* and even more specially in a film he did not sign as director, *King, Queen and Knave* ... he waged a struggle to communicate his sensibility to a wider audience. Except in *Eternal Thirst,* he failed to do so; yet in the process he introduced something of a personal cinema into the song-dance melodrama framework of commercial cinema." 'India: House Full, No Intermission', Chidananda Das Gupta in *Being and Becoming: The Cinemas of Asia,* Macmillan, New Delhi, 2002, p. 134.

Page 38 (reference to 'M. Sadiq' in line 1): "Waheeda Rehman: When Guru Dutt started *Chaudhvin ka Chand,* he could have directed the film himself, but he thought because the film had a Muslim setting, it should be directed by a Muslim director. In those days,

Sadiq Sahib had a lot of financial problems, and Guru Dutt wanted to help him so he gave him this film to direct." GDLC, p. 104.

Page 38 (lines 1-4): GDLC, p. 104.

Page 38 (lines 4-6): "Guru Dutt never denied Alvi's role in the film; nor did he make any counter claims when Filmfare's Best Director award for 1962 was awarded to Abrar Alvi. It is ironic that Guru Dutt himself never received any awards for the films he did sign as director. Since *Sahib Bibi aur Ghulam* is deeply imbued with Guru Dutt's style, it is difficult to believe that Guru Dutt, being an experienced director as well as both producer and actor in the film, did not take over its direction. Abrar Alvi has always stated that Guru Dutt did direct the songs in the film, but not the film in its entirety." GDLC, p. 120.

Page 39 (reference to 'master antinomy' in line 15): Peter Wollen, a structuralist auteur theoretician, has suggested that the work of a critic is to unearth the antinomies that constitute the works of auteurs. See, for instance, his analysis of John Ford: "The master antinomy in Ford's films is that between the wilderness and the garden." 'The Auteur Theory', Peter Wollen in *Theories of Authorship: A Reader*, John Caughie (ed.), Routledge and Kegan Paul, London, 1981, p. 140.

Page 40 (last line) - page 41 (lines 1-5): 'On the politique des auteurs', Andre Bazin in *Cahiers du Cinema,* Jim Hillier (ed.),Vol. 1, Routledge and Kegan Paul, London, 1985, p. 258.

Page 41 (lines 9-17): 'Authorship and Hollywood', Stephen Crofts in *The Oxford Guide to Film Studies,* John Hill and Pamela Gibson (eds.), OUP, New York, 1998, p. 315.

Page 42 (lines 12-18) - page 43 (lines 1-2): V. K. Murthy, interviewed by Govind Nihalani, *Encyclopedia of Hindi Cinema,* Gulzar, Govind Nihalani, Saibal Chatterjee (eds.), Encyclopedia Britannica, New Delhi, 2003, p. 500.

Page 44 (reference to 'production' in line 14): "Y.G. Chawhan: For *Sahib Bibi aur Ghulam*, Abrar Alvi sat with me. Abrar worked so hard on that film but he never got any credit. People say it was produced by Guru Dutt, so it had to be Guru Dutt's film." GDLC, p. 120.

Page 44 (reference to 'motif' in line 17): During the structuralist turn of the auteur theory, one of the methods adopted was the defining of motifs intrinsic to the structure of an auteur's body of work: "... one essential corollary of the theory as it has been developed is the discovery that the defining characteristics of an author's work are not always those that are most readily apparent. The purpose of criticism becomes therefore to uncover behind the superficial contrasts of subject and treatment a structural hardcore of basic and often recondite motifs. The pattern formed by these motifs, which may be stylistic or thematic, is what gives an author's work its particular structure, both defining it internally and distinguishing one body of work from another." Visconti, Geoffrey Nowell-Smith, reproduced in *Theories of Authorship: A Reader*, John Caughie (ed.), Routledge and Kegan Paul, London, 1981, p. 137.

Page 53 (reference to Foucault in line 6): "Foucault's attention to the relations between discourse, power, and subjects directs him rather to a concern with the conditions of existence of discourses, including those of authorship. He theorizes the author as a function of the circulation of texts. Institutions of authorship allow an author-name, which labels a given body of texts, to be disengaged from any author as expressive individual." 'Authorship and Hollywood', Stephen Crofts in *The Oxford Guide to Film Studies*, John Hill and Pamela Gibson (eds.), OUP, New York, 1998, p. 319.

Page 54 (reference to the word 'oblique' in line 10): Mikhail Bakhtin, the well-known Russian philosopher of culture, is widely believed to have written three important critical works in the 1920s one under his own name, and the other two under the names of his two friends, V. Voloshinov and Pavel Medvedev. All of them suffered under Stalin's cult of personality. In the 60s, Bakhtin was 'rediscovered' and his works came to be known world-wide. Till his death in the 70s, however, he never claimed either of the books under his friends' names to be his own. Writers on Bakhtin often use the sign of the 'oblique' to designate the authorship of the two books: Medvedev/Bakhtin and Voloshinov/Bakhtin.

Page 58 (reference to 'homelessness' in line 2): 'Homelessness' is a concept proposed by Madan Gopal Singh that links itself to thinking set in motion by the Sufi-Bhakti tradition in the subcontinent. In 'The Homeless Image: Some Preliminary Notes' in *Film and Philosophy*, K. Gopinathan (ed.), University of Calicut, 2003, Singh analyses *Sant Tukaram* as a film that questions the centrality of 'home' as a topographical and philosophical construct in the cinema. I propose that Dutt's works too can be analysed in the light of this concept.

Page 60 (lines 4-5): *Charles Baudelaire: A Lyric Poet in the Era of High Capitalism*, Walter Benjamin, Verso, London, 1983, p. 69.

Page 60 (lines 10-14): Ibid., p. 37.

Page 60 (lines16-18) - page 61 (lines 1-5): Ibid., p. 54.

Page 70 (lines 5-8): 'Streetwalking in Plato's Cave', Giuliana Bruno in *Feminisms in the Cinema*, L. Pietropaolo and A. Testaferri, Indiana University Press, 1995, p. 157.

Page 71 (reference to the word 'terrace' in line 9): "Lalitha remarks how impressions and experiences in one's own life return transformed in one's own work. Each of the Padukone's feelings for Calcutta lives on. Lalitha points to an early painting showing the confining walls of a roof terrace, typical of the architecture of Calcutta, and adds that Guru Dutt used a similar background for the *Pyaasa* song, *aaj sajan mohe ang laga lo:* '....In those days, in Calcutta, Baul singers performed on the streets. I remember that we never gave them coins, but a handful of rice. They would walk by our house in Bhowanipur, walking along with their *ektara* and singing devotional songs. Guru Dutt had used the Baul style of singing in *Pyaasa*, but he has picturised instead a woman singing *aaj sajan mohe* whereas in Calcutta the Baul singers are usually men.' " GDLC, pp. 8-9.

Page 75 (reference to 'ambivalent signifiers' in line 8): This image for me, in his saturation of grain, shimmer and emotion, calls up images from Andrei Tarkovsky's *Stalker*, 1979 and from *Solaris*, 1972 (the sequence where Chris Kelvin's mother appears when he is bed-ridden with high fever, cleans his dirtied hands and asks why he does not take care of himself).

Page 77 (reference to 'sunset' in line 1): "Abrar Alvi: I believed that Vijay should not leave and go away in the last scene of the film, but that he should stay and fight the system. I told Guru Dutt, 'Wherever Vijay goes he will find the same society, the same values, the same system'. We discussed the scene at length, but I was overruled by Guru Dutt. So I wrote the ending in which Vijay comes to Gulab and tells her to go away with him to a place from where he will not need to go any further. I asked Guru Dutt, 'Where does such a place exist in this world?' But Guru Dutt put his foot down saying, 'I like it. It's sunset, they walk away into the distance hand in hand. It will be emotionally satisfying to the audience.'" GDLC, p. 87.

Page 79 (reference to contrast between Jaba and Choti Bahu in lines 4-8): For a discussion on the contrastive representation of the two women, see 'In the Realm of Shadows', Arun Khopkar, *Journal of Arts and Ideas*, January-March 1983.

Page 91 (reference to the 'this play' in line 5): V.K. Murthy says: "Guru Dutt was the first to use the establishing shot, followed by close-ups. Thereby the expression of the actors is highlighted and the story becomes immediately intimate, more like cinema, less like theatre. He was also the first to use long focal-length lenses, such as 75mm and 100mm. This lens is useful for close-ups, it has the effect of creating movement. He was willing to take risks, to introduce new styles." GDLC, p. 84.

Page 92 (reference to 'British cinema' in line 16): "I worked with Mr. Fali Mistry from whom I learned a lot about lighting, mostly the glamorous side of lighting. But when I started seeing Hollywood and British films, I was very impressed, especially with films like: *Oliver Twist*, *Great Expectations*, *Hamlet*, and *Odd Man Out*. I was so impressed that I actually started lighting in that style when I became an independent cameraman. While the Hollywood style was quite glamorous, it did not have much realism. British films used more contrast, more realism." V. K. Murthy, interviewed by Govind Nihalani, *Encyclopaedia of Hindi Cinema*, Gulzar, Govind Nihalani, Saibal Chatterjee (eds.), Encyclopedia Britannica, New Delhi, 2003, p. 495.

Page 94 (reference to ; 'diegetic and non-diegetic space' in the last line): "The film has a dual though interwoven mode of unfolding. It is as much a film about doomed love as about the act of filmmaking itself. There are inexorable convergences and withdrawals on the multiple personae of the lovers. In this respect, the moving crane assumes an amazing mobility within the cinemascopic opening. It moves now with the ferocity of a swoop, now with the indifference of grand withdrawal. The artists and the lovers emerge through unbroken shifts in space, both inside and outside the film being made. Guru Dutt, the director of *Kaagaz ke Phool*, is also the director within the fictional space. And a lover as well!" 'Kaagaz ke Phool', Madan Gopal, Singh, *Cinemaya 13*, 1991, p. 58.

Page 101 (reference to 'movement' in line 5): "To Guru Dutt's great credit, it may be said that he not only tried to be original but almost intrepid in his use of light. For the first time he tried the idea of light as movement by creating multiple light perspectives in the same sequence-shot, at times in the same image.... It was also through this multiple flux that he would destroy the spatial claustrophobia of the expressionist films of the 30s." Ibid., p. 60.